HOME REPAIR
AND IMPROVEMENT

OUTDOOR
STRUCTURES

BY THE EDITORS OF
TIME-LIFE BOOKS

TIME-LIFE BOOKS
AMSTERDAM

TIME-LIFE BOOKS

EUROPEAN EDITOR: Kit van Tulleken
Assistant European Editor: Gillian Moore
Design Director: Ed Skyner
Chief of Research: Vanessa Kramer
Chief Sub-Editor: Ilse Gray

HOME REPAIR AND IMPROVEMENT

EDITORIAL STAFF FOR OUTDOOR STRUCTURES
Editor: William Frankel
Assistant Editor: Stuart Gannes
Designer: Anne Masters
Picture Editor: Adrian Allen
Associate Designer: Kenneth E. Hancock
Text Editors: William Forbis, John Manners, Brian
McGinn, Bob Menaker, Ellen Phillips
Staff Writers: Megan Barnett, Thierry Bright-Sagnier,
Stephen Brown, Alan Epstein, Steven J. Forbis, Lydia
Preston, Brooke Stoddard, David Thiemann
Art Associates: George Bell, Mary Louise Mooney,
Lorraine Rivard, Richard Whiting
Editorial Assistant: Susanne S. Trice

EUROPEAN EDITION
Series Director: Jackie Matthews
Text Director: Charles Boyle
Editor: Neil Fairbairn
Writer-Researcher: Susie Bicknell
Designer: Paul Reeves
Design Assistants: Andy Monks, Mike Snell
Sub-Editors: Frances Dixon, Hilary Hockman

EDITORIAL PRODUCTION
Co-ordinator: Nikki Allen
Assistant: Maureen Kelly
Editorial Department: Theresa John, Debra Lelliott

THE CONSULTANTS: Leslie Stokes was a self-employed carpenter and joiner
for seven years, specializing in purpose-made joinery and internal
fittings. Since 1976 he has taught in the building department at the
Hammersmith and West London College.

Paul Davis, a member of the Guild of Bricklayers, has been teaching at
the Hammersmith and West London College since 1979.

James H. Pendleton is construction superintendent and chief landscape
designer for a nursery in northern Virginia. His work has been exhibited
at the Washington, D.C., Armory Flower Show.

Contents

Laying the Groundwork

The basic tools. A pick and shovel for moving earth, and stakes and string for making guidelines, are the tools to start most outdoor construction. Simple hand tools like these serve for all but the most extensive earth-moving projects, but unless you are accustomed to swinging a heavy pick, schedule your digging work by instalments to avoid hand blisters and backaches.

Whatever the shape, size or conformation of the land around your house, you can probably improve both its looks and its usefulness by adding a few easy-to-build yet sturdy and handsome outdoor structures. Tool sheds and garages protect belongings; pergolas, gazebos and garden ponds add comfort and charm. Fences and walls not only ensure privacy and define boundaries but, with artful geometry, provide attractive backdrops; they also, through skilful placement, moderate the force of the wind and the flow of frost.

The land itself can be remoulded to create more pleasing contours, to improve drainage, to halt erosion or to prepare the way for the foundation of an outdoor structure. Most such construction starts with either levelling or excavating—or both—and may even involve a little surveying, a fascinating and easily mastered technique. Earth-moving requires a fairly intimate knowledge of both the surface and the subsurface of the property. Before you start building, find out whether local building and planning regulations dictate drainage patterns or fence heights, and make sure that no existing or projected road improvements will affect your work. In any case, property lines, septic tanks and underground power lines, water and gas pipes always must be marked out before any excavation work begins. Water, gas and electricity boards will stake out the locations of their lines and pipes on request. To ensure that the ground is strong and stable enough to support a planned structure, seek the advice of your local building department.

The techniques and materials described in this book are not as complex or as costly as those used on a home. The exterior concrete slabs shown here, for example, are reinforced with steel mesh, but in most cases they are thinner than those poured for a house, and many light structures can rest on pre-cast piers or, like some greenhouses and fence posts, may be set directly in or on top of the soil.

The structures themselves are similarly simple to construct. Many are open, designed to direct and encourage a pleasing flow of light and air. For such buildings, an unusual variety of construction techniques is available: post-and-beam, for example, allows the builder to use 75 to 150 mm-thick members that can bear tremendous loads and are spaced at greater intervals and with somewhat less precision than is found in residential framing. A-framing, where walls and roofs are identical, is also convenient, while domes, built like bubbles without interior bracing, are ideal for areas where posts, beams and studs would be impossible or undesirable. When you are building relatively small, open structures, these methods eliminate the need for costly framing materials and for the advanced carpentry skills and precision workmanship required for home-building. They make buildings that any amateur can put up—and be proud of.

Surveying Property with Speed and Precision

Before you start building any outdoor structure, you will need to plot its location in the most suitable area of your property. A few simple surveying techniques will enable you to set out straight lines and establish levels and angles in order to carry out this essential preparatory work as accurately and quickly as possible.

Distances can be measured reasonably accurately with string, wooden stakes, a long tape measure and a roll of light-gauge wire. A professional water level or a water-filled length of transparent garden hose makes a precise tool for determining heights or slopes and establishing level points; however, when exact measurements are not really essential, a straight-edge and spirit level or an inexpensive line level—a small spirit level designed to be suspended from a string—will adequately serve the same purpose. A ball of string and a tape measure are all you require to set a right angle.

Some jobs, however, call for a degree of accuracy that can be attained only with specialized surveying instruments. To set out construction lines for walls, footings or large slabs, to measure exact angles, to set out levels—both above and below ground—or to measure exact height differences, the most convenient tool is an automatic level, a simple yet precise surveying instrument that requires relatively little manual adjustment before it is ready to use. Automatic levels can usually be hired from surveying firms and, like any piece of precision equipment, they must be handled carefully. Do not, for example, use one on an excessively damp day: the moisture can easily affect the accuracy of the readings on the instrument.

A graduated levelling staff, which can also be hired from most surveying firms, will greatly facilitate your work with an automatic level. Commonly available in 3 metre lengths, these wooden or aluminium poles are marked with easy-to-read graduations, which are generally sharply contrasting black and white "teeth" situated at 10 mm intervals along the staff. Some sophisticated types of engineering staff come equipped with handles and a built-in spirit level as aids to vertical positioning, but generally the surveyor's assistant must use his own judgement, holding the staff directly in front of his body and bracing it firmly with a hand on each side.

A word of warning: any measurement, no matter how carefully taken, is only an approximation and even official surveys may not be totally accurate. To avoid the possibility of accidentally infringing upon your neighbour's land, always stay at least 300 mm within the boundaries of your own property when you are planning the location of any outdoor structure. If you are in doubt about the extent of your land, refer to the property deeds or consult a professional surveyor.

Simple Sighting and Levelling Techniques

Finding levels over uneven surfaces. Use a water level or improvise as here and use a transparent plastic hose partly filled with water to find on one stake or post a point that is exactly level with a mark on another. Stretch the hose between the stakes, hold one end a few centimetres above the mark you have made and ask a helper to hold the other end at about the same height. Using a funnel, fill the hose with water until the level reaches the mark. Make sure there are no air bubbles—if there are, pour off the water and re-fill the hose—then mark the second stake at the water level in the hose.

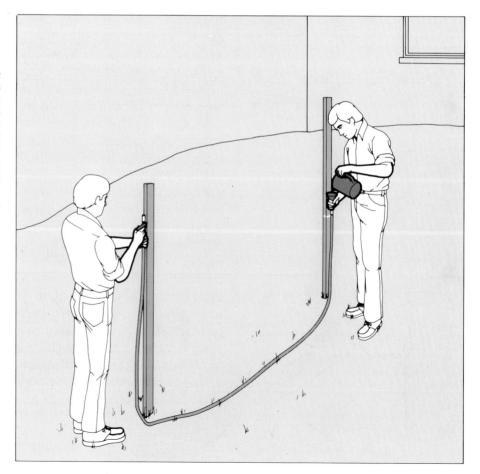

Sighting a straight line. To establish a straight line to an unseen location—in this example, a point on the other side of a hill—drive in stakes at both the starting and the unseen point. Stand at one stake, station a helper at the other and get two more helpers to hold tall poles in between, at points where the tops of the poles can be seen from both stake positions *(below)*. Sighting from your stake, signal the nearer pole-holder to move until both poles are in a straight line of sight from your position. Get the pole-holders to turn round *(bottom)*, let the other sighter do the same until the poles form a straight line from his position, then alternate sightings until the poles appear in line from both positions *(insets)*. Connect all four points with a piece of string.

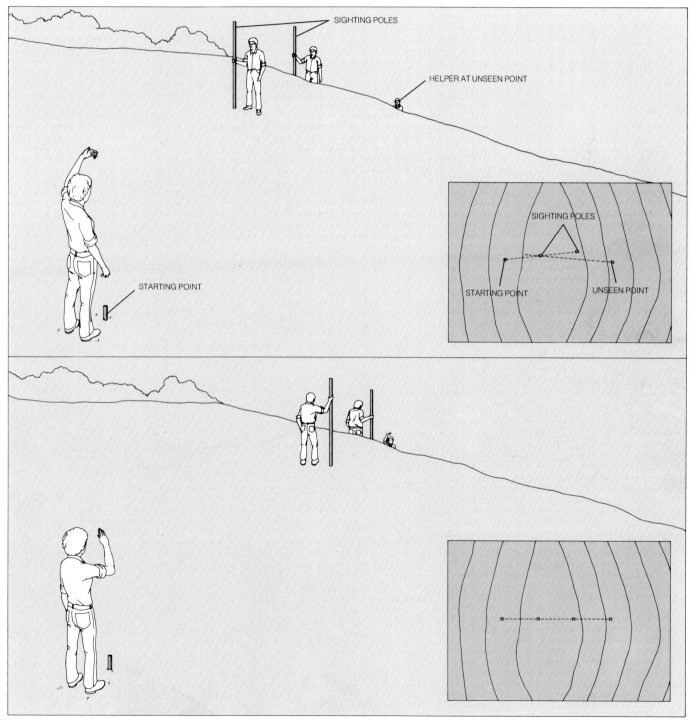

SIGHTING POLES

HELPER AT UNSEEN POINT

STARTING POINT

SIGHTING POLES

STARTING POINT

UNSEEN POINT

Setting out a right angle. Stake out the first side of the planned site and string a line between nails driven into the stakes. Exactly 900 mm from the stake (A) at which you intend to establish a right-angled corner, drive home a third nailed stake (B). Tie a 1500 mm long string to the nail in stake B and a 1200 mm string to the nail in stake A. Pull together the ends of both strings and, at the point where they meet, drive home a fourth stake (C). Stakes A, B and C should form a right-angled triangle with sides of 900, 1200 and 1500 mm; check the lengths with a steel rule and adjust stake C as necessary. Extend the line from stake A through stake C to form the second side of your planned site, at right angles to the first.

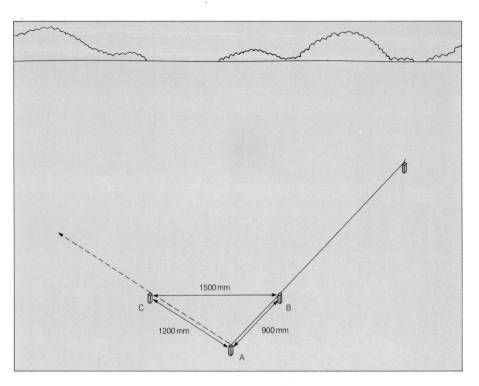

A Telescope That Measures Angles

Anatomy of an automatic level. This professional surveying tool is essentially a tripod-mounted rotating telescope with a built-in levelling mechanism and a precise scale for measuring horizontal angles. To enable you to check the instrument for level and plumb, a small spirit level is mounted on the body of the telescope and a hook for a plumb bob hangs from the head plate of the tripod *(opposite page, above)*. Three foot screws are turned to set the level, and a button under the eyepiece activates a pendulum compensator which ensures that the line of sight of the telescope is perfectly horizontal. Initial aiming is made along the sighting vane on the top of the telescope, and the object is centred precisely by turning the slow-motion screw. Cross hairs in the telescope are made sharp by focusing the eyepiece; a focusing ring is then turned to focus the object image. Stadia lines above and below the horizontal cross hair *(inset)* are used for measuring distances *(opposite page, below)*.

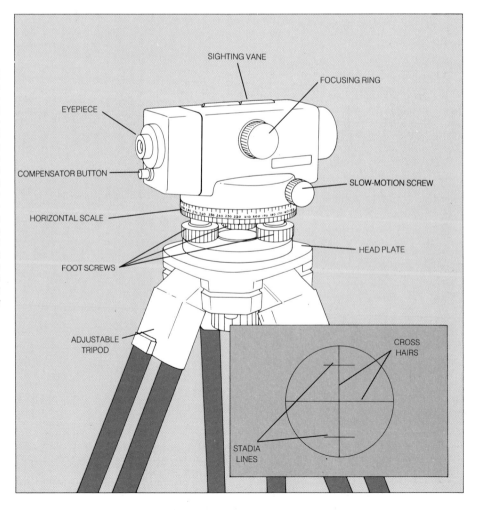

Setting Up the Automatic Level

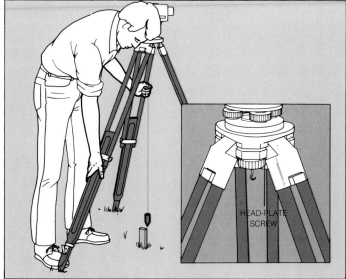

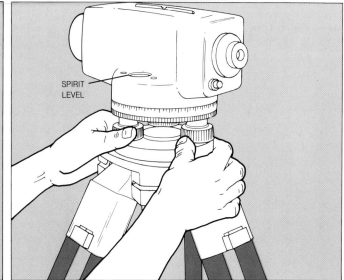

Plumbing the tripod. Spread the tripod legs 1 metre apart over a stake or other marker used as a sighting point, and move the legs one at a time until the plumb bob hangs no more than 5 mm horizontally from the centre of the stake. Loosen the screw under the head plate and shift the level on the head plate until the plumb bob hangs directly over the centre of the stake. Tighten the head-plate screw.

Setting the level. Align the telescope with two of the foot screws and turn these in opposite directions until the bubble in the level is centred. Adjust the third screw if necessary, then press the compensator button to ensure that the line of sight is perfectly horizontal. Sight through the telescope and focus, first with the eyepiece, then with the focusing ring. Centre the object by turning the slow-motion screw.

Measuring Heights, Distances and Angles

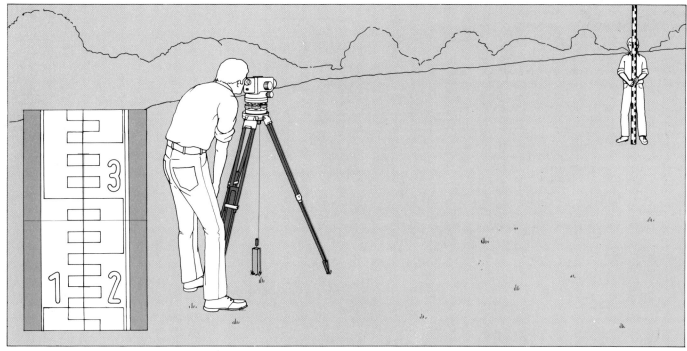

Reading a levelling staff. When determining the difference in height between two or more points, a graduated staff is used with the level to note precise measurements. While a helper holds the staff upright at the point where you wish to take a reading, focus the level and read the scale. Each tooth on the scale represents 10 mm; the reading in the inset above is 1.28 metres.

To calculate the distance between the level and the staff, subtract the reading at the lower stadia line from that at the upper stadia line and multiply by 100. In the inset example above, the difference between the stadia line readings is 0.12, which means that the distance between the staff and the level is 12 metres.

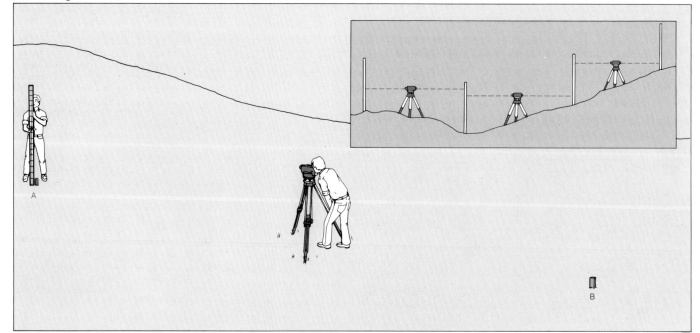

Setting a right angle. Stake out one side of the planned site. Position the automatic level above a stake (A) at the point where you wish to make the right angle, and ask a helper to hold a long pole or a graduated staff at the opposite end of the line (B). Centre the pole in the level's sights, then set the horizontal scale under the eyepiece to 0 degrees and rotate the telescope to the 90-degree graduation. Get the helper to move the pole or graduated staff until it is centred in the level's sights once more, and mark this point with a third stake. Check that the angle is accurate by rotating the level back again through 90 degrees, to point B.

Levelling Above Ground

1 **Calculating differences in height.** Mark the two points between which you wish to establish the height difference with stakes (A and B). Set up the level about half way between them. Ask a helper to hold a graduated staff at stake A and take a reading—known as the backsight—then ask the helper to move the staff to stake B and take a second reading, known as the foresight. Subtract the lower reading from the higher to find the difference in height between the stakes.

To calculate height differences over long distances or between two points that differ in height by more than the length of the graduated staff, carry out the same operation in stages *(inset)*. Record backsight and foresight readings in different columns, then add up the separate totals. To obtain the height difference, subtract the lower total from the higher one.

2 **Setting out the level.** At the lower point (B), knock in a stake so that it protrudes the same distance out of the ground as the difference in height between the two points. To check for accuracy, place the automatic level approximately midway between the two points; a backsight to point B, with the staff resting on top of the stake, should give the same reading as a foresight to point A with the staff on the ground. Run a string between the top of the stake at point B and ground level at point A to establish a level guideline for your construction work.

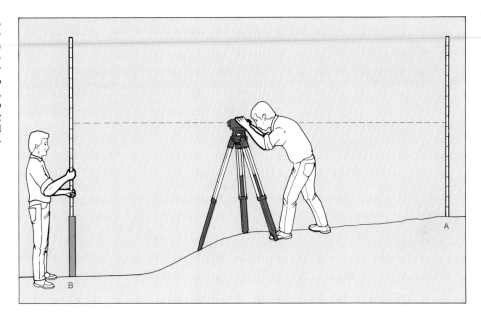

A

B

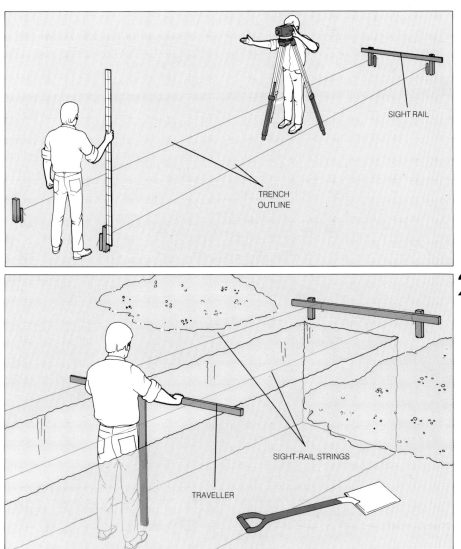

SIGHT RAIL

TRENCH
OUTLINE

SIGHT-RAIL STRINGS

TRAVELLER

Levelling Below Ground

1 **Fixing sight rails.** Mark the outline of the planned trench with chalk lines or strings run between pegs at ground level. At each end of the marked area, drive two 1 metre-long stakes into the ground. Set up the automatic level approximately midway along the trench. Mark one stake 500 mm above the ground, get a helper to hold a graduated staff against the stake with its base at the marked line, and take a reading. Get the helper to adjust the staff against each of the remaining stakes in turn until the same reading is obtained, and mark each stake at the base of the staff. Nail a 50 by 25 mm sight rail across each pair of stakes with its top level with the marks. Check the sight rails for level by resting the staff on the centre of each rail and taking readings, which should be equal.

2 **Levelling the trench.** Run parallel lengths of string between the sight rails. Nail together two straight pieces of timber in a T-shape to make a "traveller"; the crosspiece must be slightly wider than the trench width, and its height must equal the depth from the top of the sight rail to the bottom of the trench.

When you have dug out the trench to nearly the required depth, test it along its entire length with the traveller *(left)*. You will have reached the correct depth when the top of the traveller is level with the strings between the sight rails.

Your Land Reshaped to Suit Your Needs

Flattening a stretch of land, creating subtle drainage gradients, controlling the runoff of surface water—these necessary grading jobs may sound vague and ambitious. They become exact and easy when you use the professional earth-moulding techniques shown on the following pages. Moreover, you can do most of the work with plain hand tools.

Grades, which are areas smoothed and sloped for drainage, are made in two types. In one type a pair of fixed points, such as the street and the garage entrances at the opposite ends of a drive, determine the slope. In the other type, the surface of the ground is sloped just enough to drain off excess rainwater, as may be necessary in a formal lawn, a patio or a setting for a garden structure.

To set a grade having two fixed points, you must begin by measuring the difference in elevation—that is, the rise—between the points. The preferred ratio of the rise to the horizontal distance between the points varies, from 1 in 10 for an entrance path to 1 in 7 for a drive, and a maximum of 1 in 3 for a grassy bank. If you find

that the grade is too steep, you must build a solution into the site—you could add steps to a path, for example, or build a retaining wall for a lawn. For a grade as nearly level as possible, the standard minimum is 20 mm of rise for each metre of horizontal run—or 1 in 50. In porous soil, where drainage is less of a problem, 10 mm of rise is sufficient.

You can make these minimal grades by the string-and-grid method shown in these pages. The grid can also establish an exact plane for a slope between fixed points—for example, the top and bottom of a drive. But you can dispense with the grid when grading a lawn between such fixed points as the foundations of the house and a pavement if the land has a slope of 125 mm or more in each metre of run (1 in 8). In this situation your eye and your judgement will serve to make the grade sufficiently flat.

Grades are the major factor in the drainage of your property, and establishing grades that drain well must take priority over the cosmetics of landscaping. But professional land-shapers use other ways to drain land—by slowing fast runoff, by

diverting water from areas that are particularly vulnerable to water damage and by draining water from any area in which it tends to collect.

Use a double-ended pick with a point and a mattock to loosen earth for grading and drainage. A plain shovel with a long handle serves best for the digging. If you buy or hire a wheelbarrow for the job, get one with pneumatic tyres. Power cultivators with rear tines, available at tool-hire shops, are comparatively expensive, but they till better and can be guided more easily than front-tine machines. Clear away any large stones, bricks or rubble before using a power cultivator.

The fastest and easiest way to compact land is to roll it in two directions with a roller. But a roller is not sufficient if you have to fill; then it will be necessary to tamp the earth with a hand tamper or a power-driven machine tamper after putting down each 100 to 200 mm layer of soil or gravel. You must also tamp down the slopes and tops of earth terraces and any area of soil that will lie under paving slabs or a layer of gravel.

Making a Smooth and Sloping Grade

1 Establishing a rough grade. With a pick and shovel, cut down all mounds and ridges, moving the earth into holes and valleys. If the slope runs in a different direction from the planned grade, use a wheelbarrow to move earth from the high side to the planned new high side. As you work, either bury debris such as weeds, wood scraps and stones in a hole or pile it up to be taken away later. When you have finished, the area should look approximately flat.

2 Tilling the soil. Use a power cultivator to break up clods and make the earth easy to rake. Set the machine for deep tilling and till back and forth across the width and the length of the plot, making tight turns by releasing the drive clutch and swinging the cultivator round on its wheels (or, for a front-tine cultivator, on its tines).

3 Setting the slope of the grade. Drive stakes at the corners of the area to be graded. At one of the upper stakes tie a string 150 mm above the planned high edge of the grade, stretch the string to the lower stake on the same side and level it with a line level. A helper to check the level will speed up this procedure. Mark the lower stake at the string. For a minimal grade, as here, measure 20 mm down from the mark for each metre of string, and tie the string at that point. Tie level strings, from the first string to the stakes on the other side, and complete the boundary with a fourth string. For a grade with two fixed points, dispense with the line level: tie the first string to the upper and lower stakes 150 mm above the fixed points, then complete the boundary.

To measure the rise of a grade for planning purposes, tie the string at ground level on a stake at the area's upper edge and measure directly from the string to the ground at the lower edge or use an automatic level *(page 12)*.

4 **Making a grid.** Drive stakes at 1500 mm intervals along the boundary strings and connect each opposite pair of stakes with string at the desired grade to make a grid. If any grid string touches the ground, scoop out the earth underneath it to form a trench.

5 **Establishing the finish grade.** Working under and between the strings, use a shovel and a rake to move the earth into a flat surface parallel to the plane of the grid; judge by eye to see that the middle of each 1500 mm square is level with the sides under the strings. Add or remove soil as needed to bring the area exactly to the planned height, then turn the rake tines up and use the back of the tool to smooth the surface. Remove the strings and stakes and compact the soil by either rolling or tamping, depending on the function of the graded area.

Halting Erosion and Improving Drainage

Generally, the problems of surface drainage on a property have two causes: erosion and boggy low spots that accumulate water. Grading can solve problems, but the topography of the site or the amount of earth that would need to be moved may make this solution impractical.

Erosion caused by water flowing rapidly down a steep slope can endanger such vulnerable features of a property as foundations, patios and valuable plants. An attractive technique for slowing the velocity of runoff water is to build an earth terrace without a retaining wall (below). Here, the water descending a short steep slope is stopped by the terrace before it can run fast enough to erode the soil. Although laborious to construct, terraces create new level areas for landscaping as well as solve erosion problems.

An isolated patch of wet ground may be improved by digging the area over thoroughly to a depth of 300 mm and adding ashes and gypsum, or organic matter such as compost and manure. For more extensive problems, however, dig out the area to a depth of 400 to 500 mm, put in a 200 mm layer of rubble followed by a 100 mm layer of gravel, and cover with good topsoil. Make this last layer slightly higher than the surrounding ground to allow for the area to settle.

A series of soggy spots over a large area such as a lawn can be dried out by laying an underground drainage system that will carry away the excess surface water. Unless there is a convenient outlet, such as a nearby ditch or stream, you will have to construct a soakaway—a large hole designed to receive runoff water. This should be located at the lowest point in the area to be drained and should be at least 5 metres from the nearest inhabited structure.

The bottom of a soakaway must always lie above the water table (the level at which the soil is permanently saturated). Dig a test hole to establish the water table before planning where to site your drainage system. Decide whether to build a solid soakaway, which is filled with rubble, or an empty soakaway, which is lined with bricks and covered with concrete (pages 18–19): a solid soakaway involves less labour but will silt up after a number of years; an empty one has a longer life and can be cleaned out when necessary.

A soakaway of about 1 cubic metre—1 metre square, 1 metre deep—is sufficient to drain a clay-based area of 300 to 400 square metres. Lighter soil requires larger dimensions, but bear in mind that it is dangerous to dig deeper than 2 metres without seeking professional advice. When planning the depth of your excavation, remember also that the useful part of a soakaway lies below the point at which the main drain enters the hole.

Many types of land drain are available; flexible perforated plastic pipes (page 19) are simple to install because they can circumvent obstacles and they are easily joined with branch fittings. If you use the traditional—and less expensive—unperforated clay pipes, leave a 5 mm gap between each section and cover the gap with bits of slate to stop silt and roots penetrating. The pipes should be set at a constant fall to the soakaway of around 1 in 100. The depth of the trenches and the distance between branch drains varies according to soil type: a depth of 600 to 750 mm and a distance of 3 to 6 metres in clay; 750 to 900 mm and 6 to 10 metres in loam.

Carry out drainage improvements when the soil is not too wet—spring is ideal, because the garden can then recover during the summer months.

Slowing runoff with a terrace. Drive stakes about 450 mm vertically above the foot of the slope at one end of the planned terrace, stretch a level string across the slope and mark the ground along the string with chalk from a squeeze bottle. Dig into the slope above the mark and deposit the soil below it. Keep the dropoff of the filled part at the angle at which the soil falls naturally and shape the dropoff in the cut part to the same angle. Form the flat part of the terrace so that a football placed on it will roll slowly to the dropoff.

Drainage For a Waterlogged Lawn

1 **Staking out the system.** Using garden twine and pegs, stake out a square for the soakaway, then lay out the herringbone system of trenches that will feed into it. The trench for the main drain should be 300 mm wide; branch trenches join the main trench at an angle of 45 degrees and are about 150 mm wide.

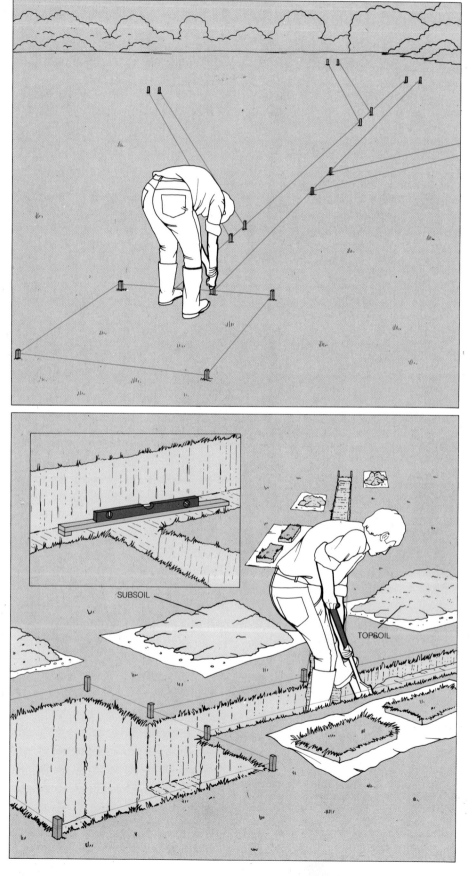

2 **Digging the soakaway and trenches.** Remove the turf and topsoil from the areas you have marked out for the soakaway and trenches; preserve both turf and topsoil on polythene sheets. Dig out a straight-sided, flat-bottomed hole for the soakaway, putting aside some of the subsoil for reuse.

Starting at the soakaway, dig out the main drain and branch trenches, setting aside the sub-soil *(right)*. The main drain should enter the soakaway as high up as possible; where the area to be drained is completely flat, lower the point of entry to allow for a constant fall for the entire system. To check the slope of your trench, pin a small block of wood to the underside of one end of a straight batten and place a spirit level on top *(inset)*—a 25 mm square block pinned to a 2 metre batten will measure a slope that is exactly 1 in 80 when the bubble in the spirit level is accurately centred.

Spread a layer of gravel 100 mm deep at the bottom of the soakaway, and spread another layer, 50 mm deep, along the trenches.

SUBSOIL

TOPSOIL

3 **Building the soakaway.** With a mortar of 4 parts sand to 1 part cement, build the interior brick walls of the soakaway, allowing 100 mm between the walls and the sides of the hole. Lay the bricks in a honeycomb pattern, leaving a 100 mm gap between each brick in a row. At the level for the entry of the main drain, build in a 500 mm length of unperforated pipe, positioning it to protrude 150 mm inside the brick wall. Build up the walls until the top course lies approximately 300 mm below ground level. Fill the space between the wall and the sides of the hole with gravel.

4 **Making a concrete cover.** Cut a square piece of corrugated metal to cover the top of the soakaway and fit flush with the outer edges of the brickwork. Construct a form round the metal sheet with 100 by 25 mm timber boards; support the form with battens nailed to the external corners and with bricks wedged between the timber and the sides of the hole.

Pour a 50 mm layer of concrete (1 part cement to 3 parts all-in ballast) over the sheet. Cover this with 6 mm 200 by 200 reinforcing mesh *(left)*, then fill the form to the top with concrete and tamp thoroughly. Remove the form after 24 hours and surround the slab with gravel. Fill up the hole to ground level with the separated subsoil and topsoil, and replace turf.

FORM

5 **Laying the pipes.** Starting from the inlet pipe built into the soakaway, place lengths of flexible piping in the trenches; use 100 mm diameter pipe for the main drain and 75 mm pipe for the branch drains, and connect the pipe lengths with fittings supplied by the manufacturer. As you progress, check with a spirit level that the slope is constant. Cover the pipes with 100 mm of gravel. To stop silt filtering through to the pipes, lay sections of turf upside down on the gravel; alternatively, use glass fibre mat or polythene sheeting. Fill the trenches to ground level with about half of the subsoil and the topsoil, then replace the turfs and press them back into position.

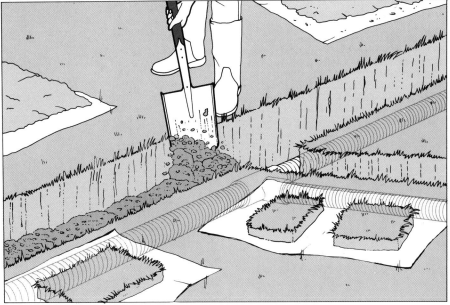

How to Terrace Slopes with Retaining Walls

For centuries farmers have turned steep hillsides into cultivable land. The technique is simple—they build an ascending series of retaining walls up a slope and fill the areas behind the walls with fertile soil until the ground is level. The same technique will serve to turn a sloping garden into a series of terraces that can be used for patios, herbaceous borders or simple lawns. Brick and stone are the traditional materials for retaining walls; concrete and concrete block are popular modern alternatives. The timber used here is easy to work with and maintain and does not require concrete foundations.

Because earth and water create tremendous pressures behind a retaining wall, you must make your wall strong and provide for adequate drainage. Begin by checking local planning and building regulations. You will need planning permission for a wall more than 2 metres high; in certain locations you must submit plans for a structure higher than 1 metre.

The next stage of planning deals with the materials you will use. For the walls themselves, you can choose between railway sleepers and timber. Sleepers are large and hardwearing, but they can be difficult to obtain and are soaked with creosote, which will quickly dull the blade of a chain saw and is poisonous to many plants. Hardwoods—oak, chestnut or elm—are naturally resistant to moisture but are expensive; softwoods, which have been pressure-treated with harmless preservatives, are both durable and inexpensive.

At the same time, choose the type and size of timber to order. Planed-all-round (PAR) timber is more expensive than sawn timber but, with its smooth surface, planed timber is easier to handle. For both types you will have to square the ends of each timber before butting it to its neighbour *(page 23, Step 4)*. Whichever timber you decide on, always buy at least 10 per cent more than your calculations indicate, to allow for wastage.

If your wall is to be a metre or more in height, use timber at least 150 mm square; for lower walls, 75 or 100 mm-square timber will suffice. Buy the longest timber that you and a helper can comfortably manage—2400 mm is a good length. And finally, plan access routes so that the timber can be stacked close to the job site when it is delivered.

At the same time, lay out routes for the delivery of drainage gravel and backfill, which you should arrange to have delivered sometime after you have completed the construction of the wall. The supplier, usually a nursery or garden centre, will advise you on the best fill for your purposes; if you are planning gardens or lawns, buy good-quality topsoil for the top 150 mm of fill. To determine how much fill you will need, calculate the volume of fill in cubic metres—the length of a wall times its height times the distance from its base to the next wall. Divide the answer in half (because approximately half the space behind the wall is already filled with existing soil), and then add 20 per cent to allow for compaction. For a drainage bed, order sufficient gravel to form a layer 300 mm wide and 300 mm deep along the entire length of the wall.

Beyond common household tools, you will need a chain saw *(page 23)*, and a heavy-duty drill fitted with a 10 mm spade bit 300 mm long. Anchor the wall to the hillside with three 1 metre lengths of 10 mm reinforcing rod for every 2400 mm of wall, and peg the layers of timbers together with three 300 mm pieces of 10 mm rod for every 2400 mm of wall. Use a hacksaw or hire a bolt cropper or cutter *(page 27, Step 3)* to cut the rods to length. If you are using 100 mm or 75 mm timber to construct the wall, the layers can be joined with 150 mm galvanized wire nails instead of with rods.

Anatomy of a retaining wall. Two timber retaining walls, each 900 mm high, terrace this hillside. Each wall consists of seven courses of 150 by 150 mm timber. The first course, buried in a trench 150 mm deep, is anchored to the hillside by 1 metre spikes made of 10 mm reinforcing rods. Succeeding courses are pinned together with 300 mm angled spikes, and overlapping timbers are spiked horizontally and vertically.

To help the wall withstand the pressure of the compacted earth behind it, each course is set 5 mm closer to the hillside than the one below, and angled into the hill. Reinforcing timbers called deadmen, 2400 mm long, run back from the wall every 1800 mm, and the free end of each deadman is attached to a crossplate spiked to the earth. As a final brace, side walls are built up on the outermost deadmen and connected to the retaining wall by interlocked corners.

To prevent water from building up behind the wall, the timbers in the second course are separated by 25 mm drainage gaps. In addition, a 100 mm perforated land drain buried in gravel routes water beyond the ends of the wall.

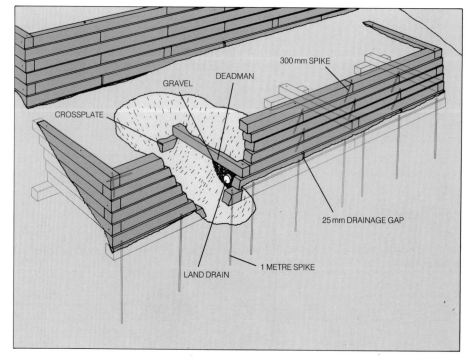

CROSSPLATE
GRAVEL
DEADMAN
300 mm SPIKE
25 mm DRAINAGE GAP
1 METRE SPIKE
LAND DRAIN

Preparing the Site

1 **Marking the wall trench.** Drive in 1500 mm stakes at the points you have chosen for the corners and tie a line between the stakes, using a water level to make sure it is horizontal *(page 8)*; then measure down from the line to find the point where the ground is lowest below the line. Mark this point with a stake.

Adjust the line between the corner stakes so that it is 900 mm above the ground at the lowest point. Drop a plumb line every 1200 mm along this line and drive in stakes at these points to mark the outer edge of the wall. String a second line along the lower stakes.

2 **Laying out a terrace.** From the upper line at a corner stake, stretch a line into the hillside and level it with a line level, then drive in a 1500 mm stake where the line meets the ground. Measure the distance between the two stakes along the ground and drive in a 1500 mm stake at this distance from the other corner stake.

Use the two uphill stakes to establish the height of a second retaining wall.

3 **Digging the trench.** Starting at the lowest point, dig a trench 300 mm wide along the line that marks the outer edge of the wall *(right)*. Measure frequently from the line that marks the top of the wall down to the trench bottom to make sure that the trench is level; for a wall 900 mm high, the trench bottom must always be 1050 mm below the string line. Remove the stakes.

With a chain saw, cut timbers to fit in the bottom of the trench, making sure that no timber is less than 1800 mm long.

Lay out deadman trenches at the wall corners and every 1800 mm along its length. For each, stretch a 2400 mm line at a right angle back from the timber and up the hill *(page 10)*, and drive a stake into the hill at the end of the line.

ADJUSTED STRING LINE   LINE LEVEL

Building the Wall

1 **Setting the tilt.** Level the first course of timbers in the trench and tilt each timber 5 mm towards the hill, propping it in position with small stones. Check the tilt with a ruler and a boat level held horizontally across each section; the gap between the bottom of the level and the top of the timber should measure 5 mm.

At the centre of each timber and 150 to 300 mm from each end, drill vertical 10 mm holes completely through the timber, using a heavy-duty drill fitted with a spade bit.

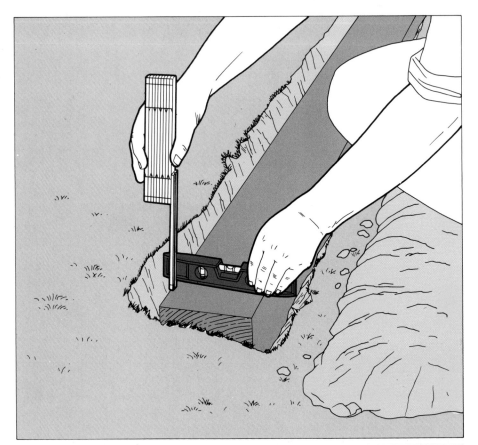

2 **Securing the first two courses.** Using a sledge-hammer, drive 10 mm steel spikes 1 metre long through the drilled holes in the timbers and into the ground. Check the level of the course and adjust the tilt if necessary. Then lay a second course of timbers upon the first, 5 mm closer to the hillside. Leave 25 mm gaps between the sections of this course, and stagger the timbers so that the gaps do not align with the joints of the first course. Drill 10 mm holes through the timbers near the ends of each section of the second course and drive 10 mm spikes 300 mm long through the holes to pin the layers together.

Dig trenches 200 mm wide and 2400 mm long along the routes you have marked for the deadmen, keeping the bottom of each trench level with the top of the second course; the deadmen themselves will rest upon the second course of timbers. For the crossplates, dig trenches 300 mm deep and 900 mm long across the ends of the deadman trenches.

3 **Bracing the wall.** Cut and lay the deadmen and crossplates. Drive 1 metre steel spikes down through the deadmen and crossplates and into the ground, and drive 300 mm spikes through the deadmen and into the second course.

To build the third course, cut squared timbers so that two lengths will fit tightly between the ends of the deadmen. Set the first timber next to a corner deadman and spike it in place.

4 **Cutting tight joints.** Set the second timber next to the first, butting the ends together, and make a cut across the butted ends with a chain saw; clean away the wood chips and push the timbers together. Drill a hole diagonally through the top of one timber, across the joint, down through the adjacent timber and into the second course of timbers below; drive a 300 mm spike through this hole to pin all three timbers together *(inset)*. Repeat this procedure until you have completed the third course. Finally, drive 300 mm spikes horizontally through the deadmen into the ends of the third course.

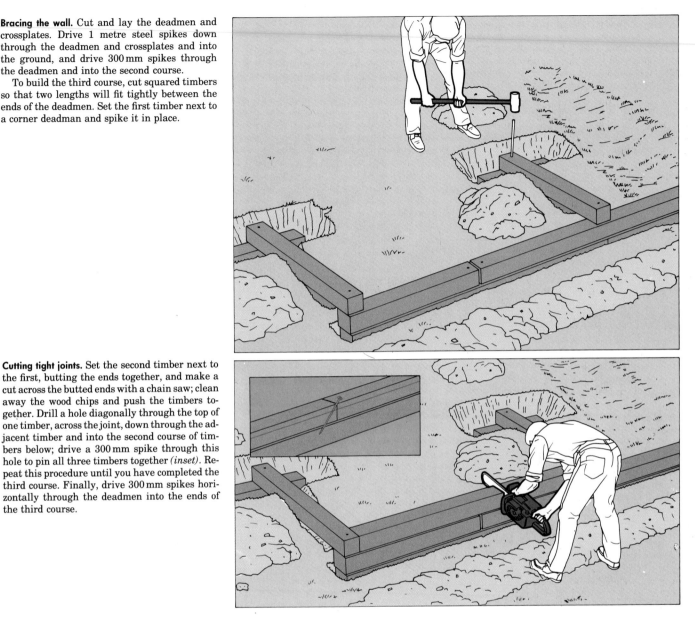

Do's and Don'ts for Chain Saws

A petrol-powered chain saw has a chain of sharp teeth that rotate round a guide bar. An automatic or manual oiler lubricates both chain and guide bar to keep them from overheating during operation. A heavy-duty chain saw can cut heavy timbers in seconds.

Chain saws must be carefully maintained and operated. When you hire one, make sure that the teeth are sharp and the chain is tight—you should never be able to pull the chain more than 3 mm away from the bar. Choose a model with

an automatic clutch—the chain will rotate only when the blade is applied to timber. Check that the saw has a safety bar and that you have sufficient fuel and lubricating oil for your job. Ask your dealer to demonstrate starting and stopping procedures and watch him cut some scrap wood. And finally, when you use the saw, follow these rules:

☐ Before cutting a timber, remove all debris from the work area, remove any nails from the wood and make sure that the timber is well supported. With a com-

bination square, mark guidelines on the timbers you plan to cut.

☐ When you start the saw, rest its body on the ground, steadying it by putting your foot on the brace which is built into the back handle on most chain saws.

☐ Use two hands to raise the saw.

☐ Make sure no one is near you when you work; always make sure that no one is behind you before you remove the saw from its cutting position. Caution: a chain saw makes a deafening noise, so it is advisable to shield your ears.

5 **Laying a drainage run.** Shovel a bed of gravel 300 mm wide and 150 mm deep along the back of the wall, and run a length of 100 mm perforated land drain along the top of the bed. At the back of the wall, nail a length of fine galvanized wire mesh over the drainage gaps in the second course of timbers, then cover both the drain and the mesh with a 150 mm layer of gravel.

6 **Interlocking the corners.** Complete the fourth course of timbers, cutting tight joints with a chain saw *(page 23, Step 4)* and spiking the timbers to the corner deadmen. Lay in the side-wall timbers and secure them with 300 mm spikes. Lay in the fifth course of timbers for the front wall and spike it in place. Then drill holes through the side-wall timbers: one vertically into the end of the fourth course, another horizontally into the fifth course. Drive 300 mm spikes through these holes to secure the corners. Using the same method, and alternating front and side-wall timbers at the ends, build the remaining side-wall and retaining courses; be sure to stagger the timber joints and to set each course 5 mm closer to the hillside than the one below.

Spread a 100 mm layer of backfill behind the wall and tamp it with a hand or petrol-powered tamper. Spread and tamp additional 100 mm layers until the fill is level with the top of the wall, then add a final layer of topsoil or gravel, sloped slightly up the hill for drainage.

Easy-to-Build Barriers of Vertical Posts

For a simple retaining wall up to 500 mm high, embed a row of vertical timbers in the ground and spike the timbers together with reinforcing rods. The wall is not as strong as a horizontal wall with deadmen, but it is considerably easier to build and useful for such small projects as tree surrounds and raised planting beds.

The top of the wall need not be level—timbers of different heights create an attractive effect—and you can, if you like, use "found" materials such as old pier pilings, telegraph poles or even logs stripped of their bark. Alternatively, use round, half-round or square treated timber. Make the basic trench for the timbers as deep as the wall is high, but at the corner posts and at every fifth timber, use a post-hole digger *(right)* to double the depth of the trench. For example, a wall 500 mm high calls for a trench 500 mm deep, but the corners and every fifth timber should be sunk in holes that are 1 metre deep.

Once the trench is dug, you need only insert the timbers one by one, starting at a corner, spike them together, fill the trench with earth and then use a hand tamper to compact the fill.

1 **Digging the trenches.** Lay out the face of the trench with a series of stakes driven in every 500 mm and dig a basic trench to the depth of the wall height. Then, straddling the corner of the trench, use a post-hole digger to make a hole twice the depth of the basic trench, for a single timber. When you have laid and pinned four timbers by the method shown below, use the post-hole digger to make another deep hole, and repeat the procedure for every fifth timber.

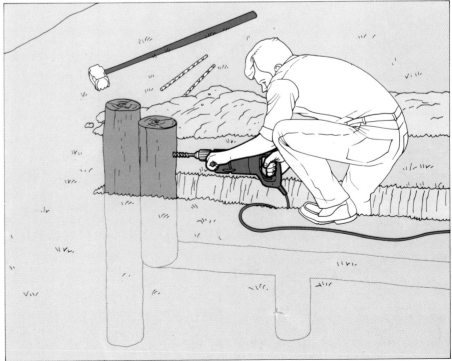

2 **Pinning the wall together.** Set the corner post in its hole, set a post next to it, and drill two horizontal 10 mm holes, one above ground level and one below, through one timber and into the next. Drive 10 mm spikes into the holes. Repeat the procedure on every post, staggering the levels of the drilled holes so that spikes do not collide.

Designing and Building a Free-Form Garden Pool

Few additions lend more charm to a garden than a sunken pool. While prefabricated pools of plastic, fibreglass or metal resist frost damage and are easy to install, they come in limited shapes and sizes. Working with concrete, you can pick the size, shape and depth that suit you—for a water garden, a fish pond or a wading pool, or for a decorative setting for a fountain or waterfall. The reinforced bowl shape of the pool on the following pages will keep the possibility of frost damage to a minimum, and it is suitable for medium to large sizes, up to about 30,000 litres capacity or 6 metres by 5 metres by 1 metre deep.

Before beginning work, check your local water authority for regulations regarding garden pools, as these may affect the size of your excavation. The local council will advise you about drainage requirements.

Choose a site free of large rocks or tree roots—to make sure, dig a series of test holes about 750 mm deep with a post-hole digger. A level site is easiest to work with, but you may prefer a slight slope—perhaps to provide a gravity drain at the low end of the pool, or to incorporate a waterfall on the high side. If you do build on a slope, you will have to provide a concrete lip on the downhill side of the pool at the same level as the upper lip, and you may have to build up the ground on the lower side to make the raised lip less obtrusive.

When you are satisfied with the location, prepare a scale drawing of the pool and take it with you to your builders' merchant for an estimate of the concrete and reinforcing materials you will need. A garden pool requires a fairly stiff mixture of concrete, consisting of 1 part Portland cement to either 2 parts sand and 3 parts coarse aggregate, or to 5 parts all-in ballast. To allow for errors, purchase about 10 per cent more of each ingredient than your estimated needs—check with the supplier to make sure that you will be able to return any unopened bags. If your plan calls for more than 1 cubic metre of concrete—the pool shown here requires about 2 cubic metres of mix—you will need to hire a mixer that you can set up at the work area.

You will also need overlapping sections of 3 mm 100 by 100 mm wire mesh to line the bottom and sides of the pool, and 6 mm steel reinforcing rods, with roughened surfaces to provide a key, to strengthen the concrete lip. Since the rods should be cut to size on the job, plan on hiring a cutter (opposite page, below, left) or a bolt cropper.

On the job itself, you will be handling several tonnes of earth and concrete; enlist helpers before excavating or pouring. Dig a hole that forms an exact bowl-shaped mould for the concrete; the bowl must rest on a base of undisturbed soil, or on a 50 mm layer of hardcore if the subsoil is clay or peat. Do not refill any part of the hole with dug-out soil; that could cause the concrete to settle unevenly and crack.

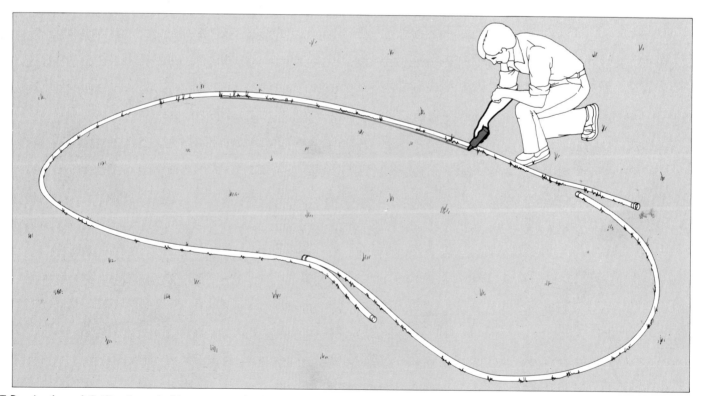

1 **Drawing the pool.** Outline the pool with a rope or a length of garden hose and transfer the outline to the ground by squirting chalk dust over the rope or hose from a squeeze bottle. Dig the hole 125 mm larger in every dimension to allow for the thickness of the concrete, and bevel the sides of the hole to a 45-degree angle.

For the construction method described here, make the hole no more than 750 mm deep.

2 **Levelling the lip.** Drive 500 mm stakes at 1
metre intervals round the rim of the pool,
150 mm out from the edge; then place one end of
a water-level hose *(page 8)* against a stake on the
upper slope, with the water in the hose 125 mm
above the ground. Ask a helper to move the other
end of the hose round the pool, marking each of
the stakes at the same level.

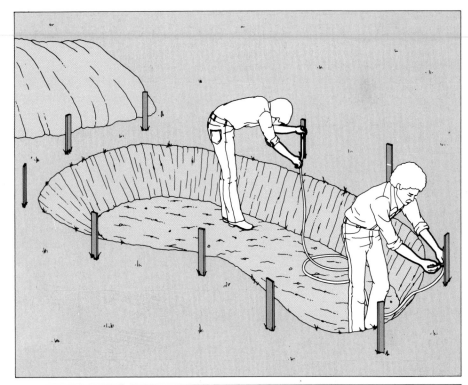

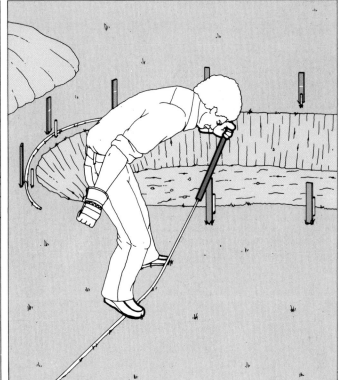

3 **Installing vertical support rods.** Cut 6 mm reinforcing rods into 500 mm lengths by inserting
the bar into a hired cutter mounted on a board
and, standing on the board, pushing downwards
on the cutter handle. Pound the rods into the
ground half way between the stakes and the edge
of the hole, bringing their tops 50 mm below the
level marks on the stakes.

4 **Bending the horizontal rods.** To shape reinforcing
rods to the curvature of the pool, slide a length of
rigid plumbing pipe over the end of a rod, step on
the rod and gradually pull the pipe towards you.
As you bend the rods, lay them in position next to
the vertical support rods, overlapping adjacent
ends by 300 mm. After bending the last rod, trim
it to size with the cutter.

5 **Making the frame.** Hold a length of the bent reinforcing rod to the tops of three adjoining vertical rods; if the bent rod does not span all three, drive in an additional vertical rod near the end of the horizontal one. Secure the bent rods to one another and to the vertical rods with short strips of soft galvanized wire *(inset)*.

6 **Fitting the mesh.** Bend sheets of 3 mm 100 by 100 mm wire reinforcing mesh to cover the bottom and sides of the pool and to extend 75 mm beyond the reinforcing rod rim. Overlap the sheets and trim the outer edges with wire cutters to fit them to the shape of the pool. When the pool and its rim are completely covered, lift the mesh one sheet at a time and place bricks underneath, on the base and sides, flat side up and spaced 300 mm apart. Secure overlaps between sheets with wire, then bend the mesh edges over the frame of reinforcing rods and tie them to the frame. To provide a depth gauge for the concrete lining, drive 400 mm pegs cut from reinforcing rods into the bottom and sides of the pool at approximately 600 mm intervals, so that they protrude by 125 mm.

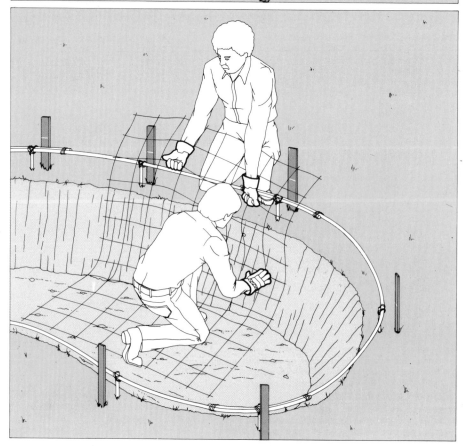

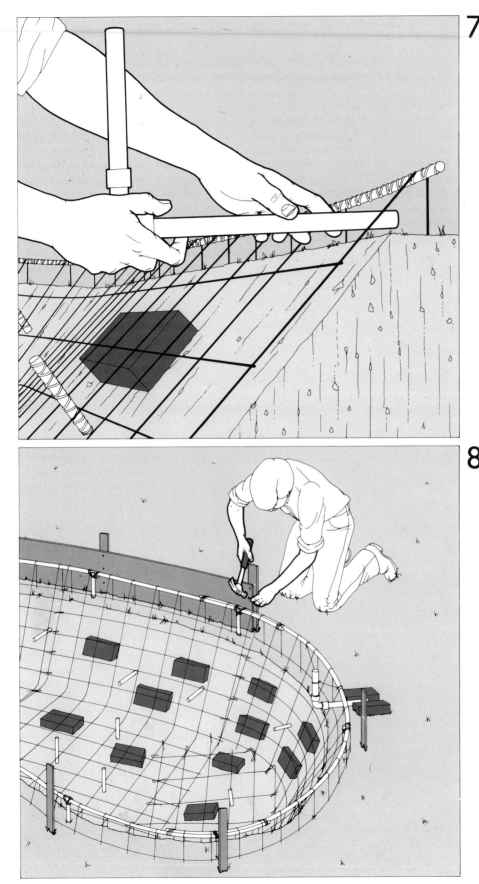

7 **Fitting an overflow pipe.** Join two 300 mm-long lengths of 18 mm plastic plumbing pipe to a 90-degree elbow joint. Insert one end through the mesh at ground level, with the elbow 125 mm inside the mesh at the rim of the pool. Turn the assembly so that the inside end points straight up. To hold the overflow pipe steady while the concrete is poured, wedge it in place with bricks or rocks and secure it to the mesh with tie wire.

8 **Making the forms.** Cut strips of 3 mm hardboard 1800 mm long and tapered to meet the level marks on the stakes; nail the strips to the insides of the stakes with their top edges at the level marks on the stakes. Notch the hardboard to fit round the overflow pipe. Brush vegetable oil or polyurethane varnish on the inner surfaces of the hardboard strips, to prevent them from sticking to the concrete.

9 **Pouring the concrete.** To support your wheelbarrow while pouring the concrete, prop a platform made of cross-braced 150 by 50 mm boards and 18 mm plywood or blockboard on cement blocks. Get a helper, standing in the pool on two scrap boards, to spread the concrete round the bottom and up the sides until the mix is even with the peg tops and the top edge of the forms.

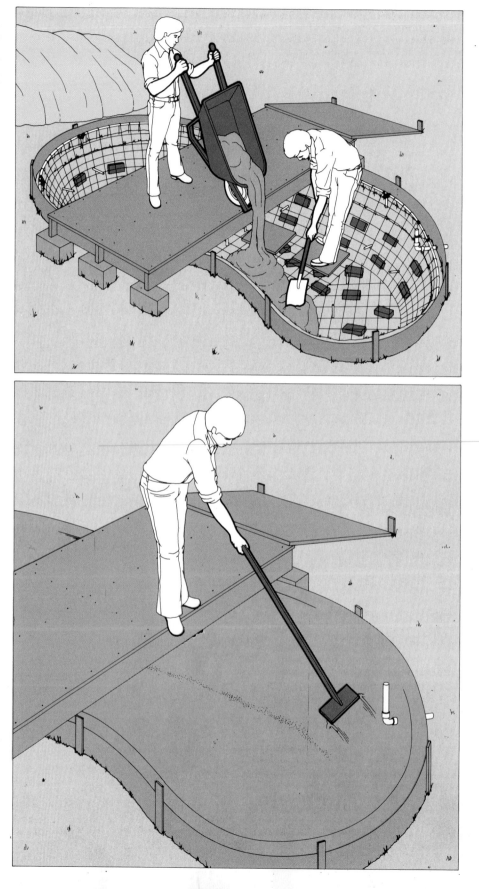

10 **Floating and trowelling.** Smooth the concrete with a long-handled wooden float, made with a 1800 mm length of 50 by 25 mm timber cut at a 60-degree angle at one end and nailed to a 300 mm length of 150 by 25 mm board. Rub the concrete lightly and evenly until all the depth pegs are just below the surface. Shape and smooth the lip with a steel float.

11 **Finishing the surface.** Draw a stiff-bristled broom across the concrete to roughen and ridge the surfaces. If the concrete has set so quickly that the bristles leave little or no impression, spray the concrete lightly with water, in order to soften it temporarily. Cover the pool with plastic sheeting well weighted down round the outer edge of the form. When the concrete has cured—this will take about a week—coat the surface with waterproof paint or a pool sealer, and plug any gaps round the overflow pipe with sealant. Saw off the top of the overflow pipe just below the rim of the pool; cover the overflow pipe intake with a circular piece of fine wire mesh, and secure it to the pipe with a plastic hose clamp.

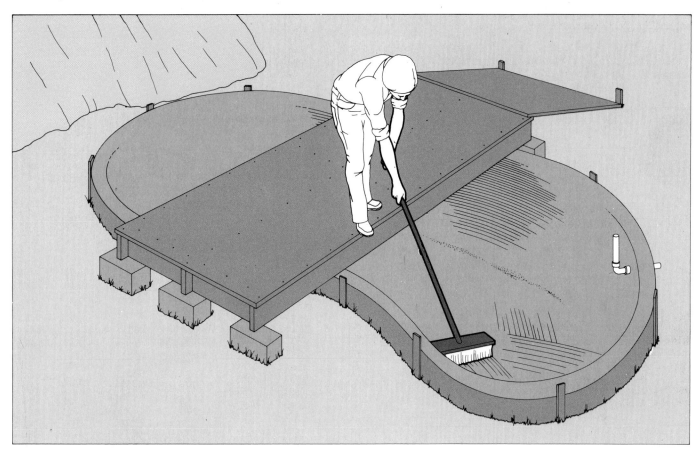

The Finishing Touches

Suppliers that stock equipment for swimming pools, gardens or aquariums sell a wide variety of materials to help you keep your pool looking distinctively attractive. Among them:

□ Plastic, vinyl or silicone paints are available in numerous colours—including black, which, to the surprise of some people, is the preferred choice of most landscape designers and offers many advantages. It looks natural and gives an illusion of great depth. And, because it absorbs heat, it helps to protect fish and plants from the shock of a sudden frost or from cold weather.

□ Pools holding more than 1,000 litres should be equipped with an electric recirculating pump to aerate the water and prevent it from becoming stagnant. There are two kinds of pump: the submersible type, placed in the pool and hidden beneath plants or a stone shelf; and the non-submersible type, generally placed in a shallow well-hole next to the pool. Pumps are rated by the number of litres of water they can circulate in one minute (referred to as LPM by pump manufacturers); a unit with a rating of 33 LPM is sufficient for a medium-sized pool of 1,000 to 3,000 litres.

□ If you plan to use your pool as a fish pond or as a setting for water plants, buy a sealing or seasoning agent from an aquarium supply shop or garden centre. This treatment neutralizes the harmful alkalis in freshly cured concrete. The alkalis can also be neutralized by filling the pool with a solution of 1 litre of vinegar to every 400 litres of water. Leave the solution in the pool for three days, then drain it off and scrub the pool thoroughly with a stiff brush. After rinsing the pool, refill it with fresh water and plant water lilies in pots set on the pool bottom, or plant water hyacinths that float on the surface. Marginals—plants such as water irises—can be set in raised containers round the edges of the pool.

□ Algae growth, a recurrent problem in still pools, can be curbed by chemical algicides, but the best solution is to grow submerged oxygenating plants such as the *Elodea* species, which consume the mineral salts that algae thrive on.

2 Borders of Wood, Brick and Iron

There are many reasons for fences, and there is a fence for almost every purpose. A tall fence can appropriately surround a swimming pool, an outdoor room, a sunbathing area or an entire garden. You can achieve either total privacy with a brick, board or panel fence, or partial privacy with a louvred, picket or board-and-board fence. In addition to providing privacy, fences can enclose areas, fend off the elements, embellish your house and land, or perform all these functions at once. Used as a boundary, a fence says, with emphasis that depends on height and construction, "Don't cross". In a friendly, unassertive way, such a barrier can keep out animals, cyclists and shortcutters, and prevent trespasses that could cause friction between neighbours.

Because property-line fences involve other people, do not build one until you are certain where the boundary runs. Refer to your property deeds and, if in doubt, employ a professional surveyor. Check also whether you will need planning permission, as regulations may establish height, or the fence's setback from a street to ensure visibility for drivers. In many places a fence built by one neighbour on a boundary line automatically becomes the joint property of both neighbours. And if you incorrectly locate a fence beyond your property, the mistake is costly to remedy. In any fence-building project near a boundary, it is wise to seek the co-operation and good will of your neighbour.

Boundary marking contributes to privacy, but fences also influence the environment—even the climate—around your house. A fence can temper the wind—although, paradoxically, a solid fence makes a poor windbreak; the flow of air over the top creates a tumbling eddy that pulls the wind back down to the ground again. An open picket, slat, louvred or lattice fence, however, will generally slow the wind and reduce its chilling effect. In some cases, open fences can be angled to funnel summer breezes, increasing their velocity so that the funnel area seems cooler than the rest of the garden. Solid fences that reach the ground dam the flow of frost—a peril to tender plants upstream of the dam but a boon to those below.

To enhance your property's appearance, choose a fence style that avoids either an exact match with the house (a horizontal board fence for a weatherboarded house) or a head-on clash. Consider matching an element of a house (brick piers and an iron fence for a classical brick house) or creating a deliberate but tasteful contrast. A plain fence can set off plantings; a handsome fence that hides a dustbin or a compost heap does double duty. Many fences look better from one side than from the other; usually you will want to show the world the more attractive side. Your neighbour will thank you, thus demonstrating once again the accuracy of the old saying: good fences make good neighbours.

Setting Fence Posts Straight and Secure

The key to a good-looking, long-lasting fence is a series of sturdy fence posts, securely anchored and properly aligned and spaced. The posts are the working members of a fence, bearing and bracing the gates and railings. But the posts are also an important element in the design of a fence, creating evenly spaced visual breaks in long runs of railings or panels.

Generally, the function and size of the fence determines the characteristics of its posts. Heavy wind-resistant fences, and any fence that is more than 1800 mm high, should be supported by posts made from timber no smaller than 100 by 100 mm. Low picket fences can be anchored with 100 by 50 mm intermediate, or line, posts but even on a lightweight fence the end, corner and gateposts should be at least 100 by 100 mm. Use pressure-treated timber, which is impregnated with wood preservative under pressure so that the entire post is resistant to rot and fungus. Pressure-treated posts last up to 20 years, while untreated posts may have to be replaced after as few as five years.

The depth of the post hole and what filling to use in it are the next considerations. As a general rule, one-third of the post should be below ground; an 1800 mm fence, for example, requires 2700 mm posts sunk 900 mm into the earth. In rela-

tively stable soil, tamped earth or gravel will hold the post securely. Concrete makes a more secure setting and is advisable in loose or sandy soils and for any fence over 1200 mm. The gateposts and the end and corner posts, which are subjected to greater stress, should be set in concrete wherever possible; however, if you prefer not to go to the trouble and expense of using concrete, use longer lengths of timber for these key posts and sink them deeper into the ground. Posts for panel fences should not be set in concrete or tamped earth until the panels are in place, to allow for any final adjustments that may be necessary.

Although concrete footings provide the most solid base, they can be subject to frost damage in colder climates. As freezing water expands under and around the footing, a phenomenon known as frost heaving tends to force the post up out of the ground. If the frost depth in your area is quite shallow, there should be no difficulty setting the posts below the frost line. In very cold climates you can minimize the problem in post holes shallower than 900 to 1000 mm, the maximum practical depth, by widening each hole at the base into a bell shape so that the surrounding earth holds the concrete in place.

The exposed end grain at each end of the post requires additional protection. To pre-

vent the bottom from resting in ground water, shovel at least 100 mm of gravel into each hole, to act as a drain. To help protect the top from rain, cut the post at a 30 to 45-degree angle, or cover it with a wooden or metal post cap, available from fencing suppliers to fit standard post sizes.

Post spacings are determined by the standardized widths of fence sections and railings; if you build your own fence, it is simpler to use standard timber sizes, to reduce cutting and fitting on the job. In general, posts should not be spaced more than 2400 mm apart; at this spacing, a 4800 mm length of timber spans three posts. After measuring the length of the fence and allowing for any intended gates, you may find that you need to use tighter spacing and shorter lengths of timber, in order to avoid ending a fence with a noticeably narrow section.

Measuring and marking post locations is a relatively simple job on flat ground; on sloping or uneven ground, the type of fence determines the measuring method. For fences that slope, measurements should be made along the surface. For fences of panels with level tops, measure spacings along a level line above the ground. On hillsides, the panels are often stepped down in level sections, with posts evenly spaced along a level line.

Where to Place Post Holes

Locating posts on flat ground. Drive in stakes at the locations of the end posts, stretch a string between the stakes, just high enough to clear the ground, and measure the length of the string to determine the standard lengths of timber or fencing that will make up the fence with a minimum of cutting. Make a gauge pole—a piece of straight 50 by 25 mm timber to cut to the length of the fence sections and marked off in 300 mm increments—and set it repeatedly on the ground against the string, to set the locations of the intermediate posts. Use the markings on the pole to adjust locations for gateposts and to avoid ending the fence with a very short section.

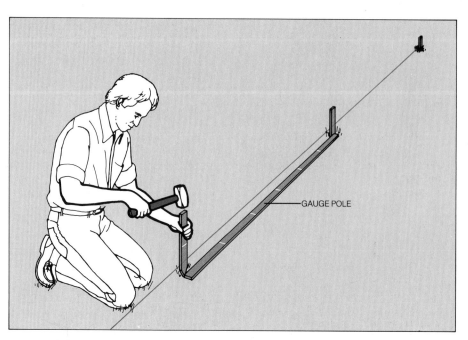

GAUGE POLE

Staking posts on uneven ground. For a fence with rigid rectangular panels, or one with a level top, such as a picket fence *(page 43)*, stretch a line between two end stakes, level it with a line level or a spirit level on a straightedge and, working with a helper, measure along it with a gauge pole. Drop a plumb bob from the line to pinpoint each post location on the ground *(below, top)* and drive in marker stakes at all the post locations. For a fence such as a post-and-board *(page 49, top)*, with a top that follows the natural contours of the ground, drive in stakes at the fence ends and at each high and low point in between. Join all the stakes with string and use a gauge pole to space the remaining posts evenly between the post locations already marked *(below, bottom)*.

To run a straight line of string over hills or in areas with heavy undergrowth or other obstructions, use the sighting techniques on page 9.

Using a post-hole digger. After removing the marker stake, use a manual post-hole digger or borer to dig a post hole. For a post set in concrete, make the hole at least three times the post width and angle the digger to widen the bottom. For posts set in tamped earth, dig a hole that is twice the post width. Make the hole about 150 mm deeper than the depth of the post below ground. Fill the bottom with 100 to 150 mm of gravel, topped with a flat rock.

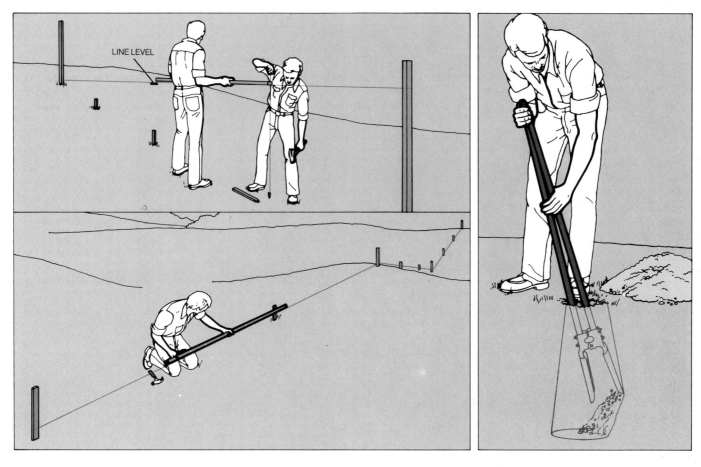

A Timesaving Tool for Digging Holes

A petrol-powered auger, available from tool-hire shops, saves both time and effort, especially if you are setting 10 or more fence posts, unless you are working in very rocky or sandy soil.

Power augers weigh between 15 and 20 kilograms and come with a removable spiral-shaped boring bit that can excavate holes up to 800 or 900 mm deep. Some models can be operated by one person, but the two-man auger shown on the right is safer to use; it is much less likely to kick out of the hole when it hits a rock or other similar obstruction.

To use a power auger, mark on the bit with tape the depth of the post hole to be excavated, and set the bit over the marked position. Start the motor, adjust the speed with the handle-mounted clutch and exert an even downward pressure from both sides. After digging a short distance, slowly raise the bit to clear the dirt from the hole. If you hit a rock, stop the motor and use a digging bar or pick and shovel to prise the rock loose. Do not use a power auger near any trees with large roots as these can cause the machine to kick out of its hole.

35

Getting your Posts in Line

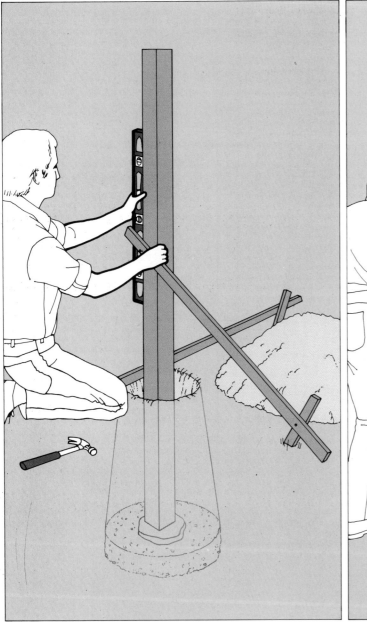

Bracing an end post plumb. Drive in two stakes on adjacent sides of the post hole and fasten a 50 by 25 mm bracing board to each stake with a single nail. Set an end post in the hole, centred over the flat rock at the bottom, and use a spirit level to plumb a side of the post adjacent to a bracing board. When that side is plumb, nail the upper end of the bracing board to the post. Then plumb the side adjacent to the other board and nail that board to the post. Brace the other end post using the same technique.

Aligning intermediate posts. Stretch two strings between the sides of the end posts, one near the top and the other close to ground level. While a helper aligns one side of an intermediate post with the two strings and plumbs an adjacent side with a level, sight along the top string to check both the post height and the alignment. To make minor adjustments in height, add or remove gravel; to alter alignment, move the rock on which the post is centred.

If the posts are to be anchored in tamped earth, fill the holes with soil or gravel and tamp (opposite page, left) as you set each post; if you are setting the posts in concrete, brace all the posts as shown above until the concrete has hardened.

Two Ways to a Secure Support

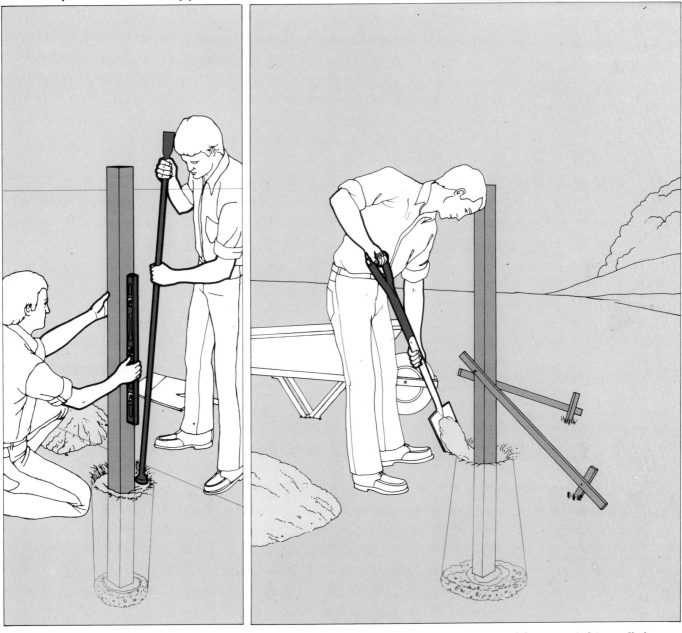

In tamped earth. While a helper holds the post plumb, fill the hole with earth, in 75 to 100 mm layers; as each layer is put in, tamp the soil with the flat end of a digging bar *(above)* or a 75 by 50 mm. Overfill the hole and shape a cone of earth round the post to channel away runoff.

In concrete. Check the braced post for alignment and plumb, then fill the hole with a foundation concrete mix—1 part cement to 2½ parts sand and 3½ parts coarse aggregate or to 5 parts all-in ballast. Overfill the hole slightly and use a trowel to bevel the concrete down from the post to provide a runoff. Within 20 minutes, recheck the post for plumb and make any small adjustments, adding additional concrete as necessary. Allow the concrete to set for at least three days before removing the braces or attaching fencing. If the concrete leaves a slight gap round the posts as it dries, caulk the space or fill it with bitumen roofing adhesive.

As an alternative, to save both concrete and the effort of mixing it, you can simply empty half a bag of dry pre-mixed concrete into the hole, on top of the gravel, and fill up the rest of the hole with earth. Although this method of securing a post is not as strong as a full concrete footing, natural seepage of ground water will eventually solidify the concrete base while the tamped earth holds the post up.

Repairing and Replacing Posts

Even the best-anchored posts will eventually require realigning, or may need replacing entirely. Posts forced slightly out of alignment by wind or frost can often be pushed back into position and secured by retamping the earth round them or by driving wooden shims between a post and its concrete base. A post that leans steeply may need to be braced by a length of steel pipe or reinforcing rod.

Damage to the upper half of a post can be repaired with a new section spliced to the base. If only the base is rotten, you can saw off the sound upper section of post and reinstate it with either a metal or a concrete support. A metal support consists of a square socket mounted on a spike 600 to 750 mm long. Drive the spike into the rotten wood below ground and slot the usable section of post into the socket. For a concrete support, dig a hole as near as possible to the side of the rotten post base, set the support in the hole and fix the upper section to it with coach bolts.

Where damage is widespread, replace the entire post. Sometimes the location of a post can be moved half a metre or so without extensive cutting of fence rails or panels; in this situation, simply set a new post in the new location and saw off the old one flush with the ground. Otherwise, you must drill and chisel out the rotten stump or, if necessary, uncover the entire footing, then break up the concrete into manageable chunks with a crowbar or digging bar and pour a new footing.

Fixing a leaning post. If wooden shims round the base do not hold a post vertical, use steel pipe and a heavy-gauge perforated metal strap or heavy-duty wire to pull the post into alignment. On the side away from the lean, drive a 1500 mm length of 38 mm pipe half way into the ground just clear of the concrete footing. Nail one end of the strap to one side of the post, loop the strap round the top of the pipe and, while a helper pushes the post back to plumb, nail the other end of the strap to the opposite side of the post.

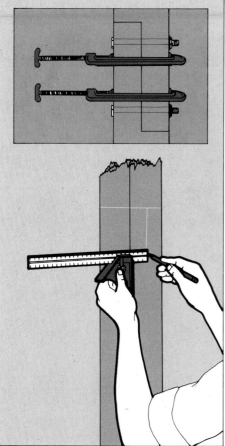

Replacing the top of a post. Use a combination square to mark a cutting line round the post below the damaged part and to draw a 200 mm vertical mark from the cutting line down the centre of one side of the post; from the bottom of the vertical mark, extend a horizontal mark to the post edge. Duplicate the marks on the opposite side of the post, cut off the damaged section and saw out the wood inside the marks for a lap joint. Cut a matching joint on the new post section and glue and clamp the joint. When the glue has set but before you remove the clamps, drill two bolt holes through the lapped sections *(inset)*; secure the joint with 100 mm galvanized bolts.

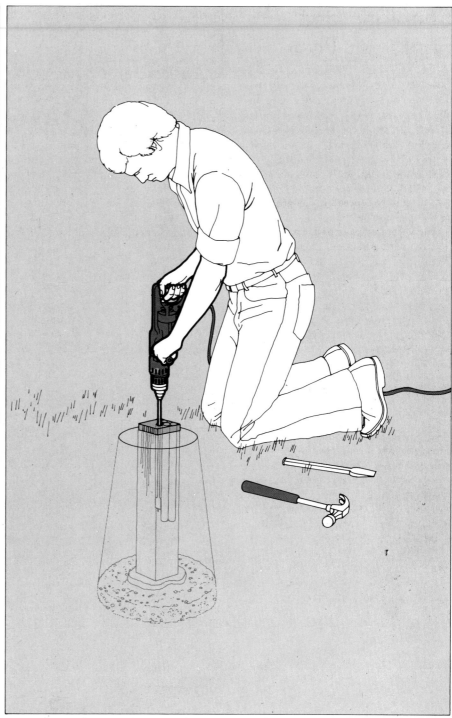

Replacing a post. Saw the post off a few centimetres above its concrete footing and drill a number of holes down into the centre of the stump using a spade bit 450 mm long in a heavy-duty drill. Keep the drill bit clear of the concrete. Use a cold chisel or crowbar to split and loosen the stump, and when all the wood is out, set the new post in the hole. If the post is too small, drive shims round the base while a helper plumbs the post; if it is too wide, taper the end with a hammer and chisel.

Wooden Fences: Variations on a Basic Theme

Almost every wooden fence is built on a framework of upright posts and connecting horizontal timbers. This simple skeleton can carry a range of fences that will meet practically any need. A fence of nothing more than posts and boards makes a clear boundary marker, adapts well to rough or rolling terrain and covers the most ground with the least timber. Boards nailed to a post-and-rail frame can take the shape of a low picket fence to decorate the border of a front garden or a tall board fence to ensure privacy or keep children and pets safe.

In all of these fence styles, your first concern is the quality of the building materials. Hardwoods such as oak and chestnut are naturally resistant to insects and decay but are very expensive; pressure-treated softwood is a less costly alternative. Make certain that any timber you use has been adequately seasoned.

If you cannot get pressure-treated softwood in the sizes you want, treat the wood yourself. Soak boards in a preservative that will not harm garden plants when dry. If you cannot soak the timber, paint it liberally with preservative, using especially heavy coats at sawn ends. While you assemble the fence, daub additional coats of preservative on fresh cuts and adjoining surfaces. When handling preservative, always wear protective gloves and, wherever possible, work away from greenery. If you intend to paint the fence, paint all of the timber before beginning to assemble it. Use stainless-steel, hot-dipped galvanized or aluminium fasteners which will not rust and stain the fence.

The basic post-and-board fence on these pages is made of 25 mm timber, face-nailed to 100 by 100 mm posts. The posts—900 to 1200 mm high for a three-board fence, 1200 to 1500 mm for a four-board one—can be topped with either metal or wooden post caps or with an angled cap rail (opposite page) to protect the ends, which rot easily, from moisture. Space the posts to use standard lengths of board as much as possible.

Post-and-rail fences, with tapered rail ends that fit into mortised posts, are sturdier than post-and-board fences and almost as easy to install. Prefabricated mortised posts and tapered rails are sold by fencing suppliers in a variety of styles. All are assembled like the split-rail fence illustrated on page 42.

Picket fences can also be built in a wide range of styles, and are available in kits. A picket fence can be constructed to any desired height but is usually between 900 and 1200 mm, with pickets projecting about 150 mm above the top rail.

The Simplest Fence of All

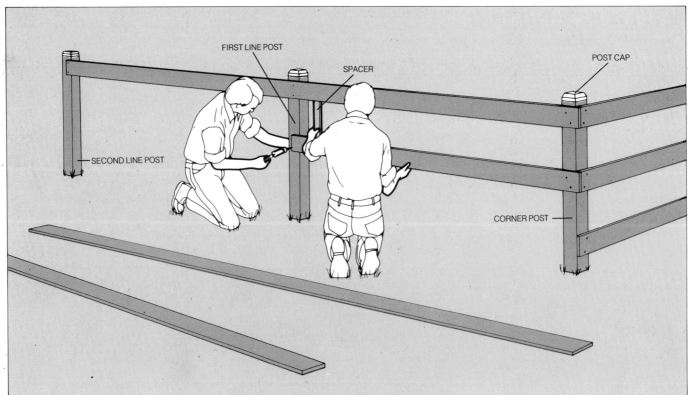

Building a post-and-board fence. To start from an end or corner, trim 100 by 25 mm or 150 by 25 mm boards to extend from a corner or end post to the centre of the second line post, and stagger these long boards with others extending only to the centre of the first line post. Nail on these boards. Use a piece of scrap wood as a spacer to position the lower boards. Continue to add long boards until you need short pieces for ends. Nail metal or wooden caps to the posts.

Desirable Extras: a Cap Rail and Battens

1 Bevelling the posts. To prepare the posts for the cap rail, saw a 30-degree angle at their ends—you can start the cut with a circular saw set to the appropriate angle *(below, left)*, but it will not cut all the way through and you must finish the task with a handsaw. To prepare a corner post, make a second cut at a 30-degree angle across an adjacent side *(below, right)*.

Set all posts in position, placing the corner ones so their bevels slant to support mitred cap rails.

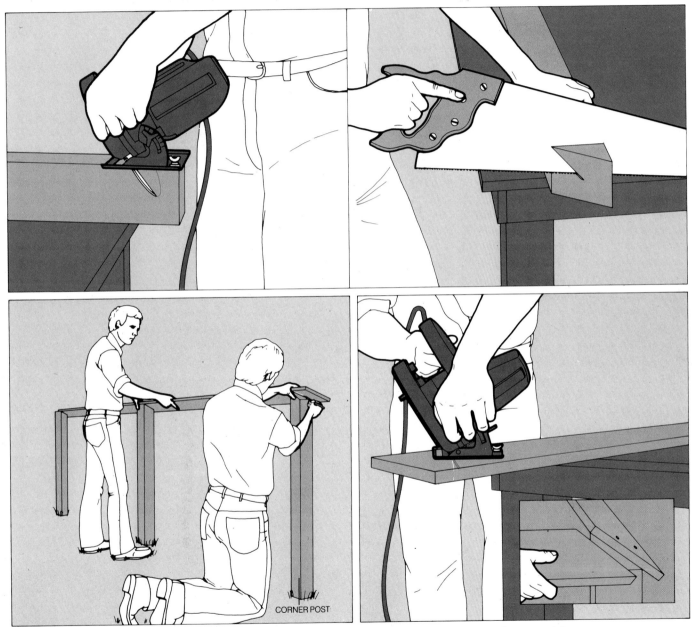

CORNER POST

2 Marking the cap rail. With a helper, hold a 150 by 25 mm in position on top of a corner post and a line post. Get the helper to set one end of the board at the centre of the line post while you mark the underside of the board along the angle of the corner-post top *(above)*. Then mark a second 150 by 25 mm cap-rail board to fit across the other angled face of the corner post. Use a steel square to transfer the marks to the other side of each board to facilitate sawing.

3 Cutting the cap rail. With a circular saw, cut the rails along the corner-post marks at 30-degree angles, bevelling the ends of the boards so that they can be mitred flush.

Nail the cap-rail sections to the corner and line posts, aligning the tops of the rails with the top edges of the bevelled posts *(inset)*.

4 **Installing the battens.** Once you have fastened all the boards, cut 25 mm thick batten boards long enough to reach from the underside of the cap rail to a few centimetres off the ground. Nail them to the posts.

Fitting Together a Rail Fence

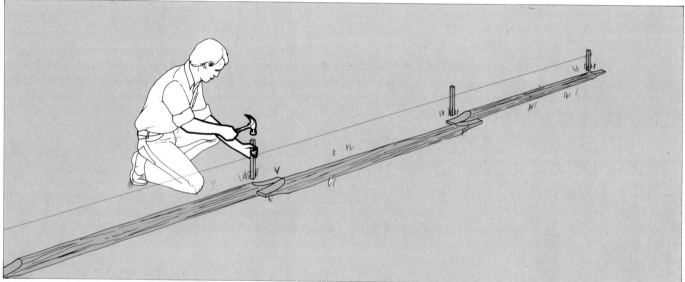

1 **A dry run of rails.** Drive in stakes for the end posts and string a line between them *(page 34)*. Lay pre-cut rails on the ground along the fence line, overlapped as they will be in the mortises of the posts—if the rails do not fit evenly, move the end stakes if possible or cut short rails for one or two sections of the fence. Drive in additional stakes at the centres of the overlaps. Dig holes for the posts at the stake locations.

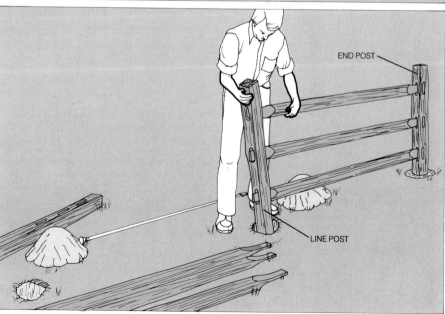

2 **Fitting the rails in place.** Set an end post in tamped earth *(page 37)* and lower the first line post into its hole; then insert the ends of the rails into the slots of the end post and, as you lift the line post upright, fit the other ends of the rails into the line-post mortises. Plumb the line post, secure it with tamped earth and set succeeding sections the same way.

Putting Up a Picket Fence

1 Installing the rails. For the bottom rails, trim 100 by 50 mm boards to fit between each pair of posts and nail galvanized 100 mm angle brackets to their ends. Attach the rails to the posts about 200 mm above the ground, nailing through the angle brackets and then toenailing.

Use long 100 by 50 mm boards for top rails to span as many posts as possible. Nail them on top of the posts, cutting them to meet in the centres of line and corner posts. At line posts, bevel the rail ends at an angle of 45 degrees so that they overlap; at corner posts, mitre the rail ends.

2 Attaching the pickets. Using a piece of scrap the length of a picket, make a spacer as wide as the distance between pickets. Nail a block of wood about 150 mm from one end of the spacer, as a cleat; hang the spacer on the fence by hooking the cleat over a top rail. Set the first picket at the edge of an end post, align its point with the top of the spacer, plumb it with a level and nail it in place. Proceed along the fence, using the spacer to locate each picket. Check with a level every few pickets, to be sure they are not drifting out of plumb. Stop about 1 metre from the end of the fence and check the fit of the remaining pickets; adjust spacing if necessary, so the last picket will be flush with the outside edge of the end post.

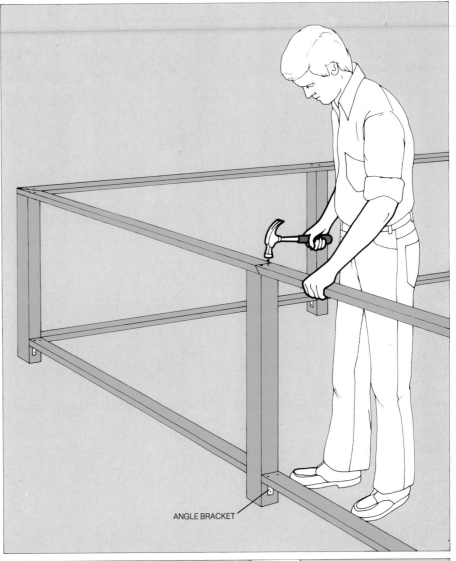

ANGLE BRACKET

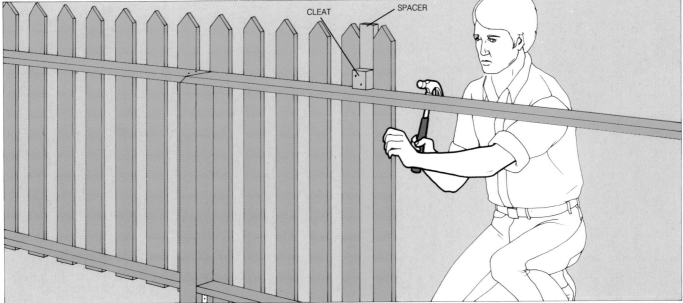

CLEAT SPACER

Pickets in Patterns

1 Building a panel. Build rectangular frames of 75 by 50 mm boards to fit between each pair of posts. Cut picket slats to the length of the longest picket in your pattern and, starting from the ends, nail several of them to the frame laid out on the ground. Align the pickets evenly along the bottom of the frame, using a spacer with a cleat that holds the spacer's end about 100 mm below the frame bottom. In the centre of the panel, lay the pickets on the frame without nailing, adjust their spacing, mark their positions on the rails and nail them in place.

2 Marking a curved pattern. Measure down from the top centre of the panel of pickets the full depth of the curve and drive in a central nail. Drive in two end nails at the top of the picket panel, each a distance from the central nail equal to half the panel length. Tie a cord to one end nail, pull it round the central nail and fasten it to the other end nail. Now remove the central nail, substituting for it the point of a pencil. Keeping the cord taut, use the pencil to draw a curve on the picket panel. Mark each panel in the same manner and cut along the curves with a jigsaw.

CENTRAL NAIL
END NAIL   END NAIL

3 Installing the panels. Get a helper to hold each panel in position against the posts so that the post top fits into the picket pattern. The bottom rail should be about 200 mm above the ground. Nail the panels to the posts through the uprights and, for additional support, toenail through the bottom rail from the side.

Tall Fences for Privacy

Although they are higher and heavier, most tall fences are built much like the picket fence on page 43. Common boards or stakes nailed to simple post-and-rail frames will produce a variety of attractive fences, prefabricated panels, which are nailed directly to posts *(page 46)*, also come in sections up to 1800 mm high.

Some fences, however, require more sophisticated carpentry. A tall louvred fence, for example, is heavier and more prone to warp than some of the simpler designs and should be made with sturdier joints. To build the louvred fence on pages 47–48, use a router to cut housings in the rails.

Where conditions are particularly damp, it is wise to protect the bottoms of vertical fence boards from decay by installing a "gravel board"—a length of 25 mm timber about 150 mm wide—along the base of the fence. Nail it to battens fixed to the inner fences of the posts, then secure the vertical boards above it. Replacing a rotten gravel board is easier than replacing an entire section of fencing.

Five Screens for Your Garden

Boards and panels for high fences. All of the fences on the right are supported by posts 1500 to 2400 mm high, set no more than 1800 mm apart. The simplest tall fence—known as the closeboard fence—is supported on a post-and-rail framework. In a vertical closeboard fence, boards are nailed directly to the bottom and top rails, and to a middle rail if the fence is taller than 1800 mm. For a horizontal version, boards are face-nailed to the posts and to 100 by 50 mm vertical supports nailed to top and bottom rails 400 to 800 mm apart. Boards can be butted together to form a flat surface, or overlapped, in which case feather-edged boards are usually used.

A board-and-board fence admits breezes and looks good from either side. Vertical boards are nailed to both sides of the frame, separated by less than their own widths. The boards on one side are positioned opposite the spaces on the other. Ready-made panels, mounted on their own framework, are available in a wide range of designs. Interwoven panels create a wind and peep-proof fence; lattice or trellis panels *(page 94)* give less protection but provide the perfect backdrop for climbing plants.

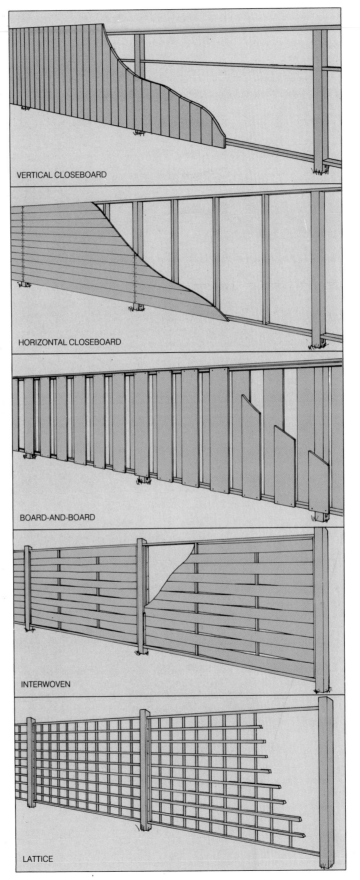

VERTICAL CLOSEBOARD

HORIZONTAL CLOSEBOARD

BOARD-AND-BOARD

INTERWOVEN

LATTICE

A Tall Fence of Prefabricated Panels

1 Positioning the end post and panel. Locate and dig holes for the posts and brace the first post plumb *(page 36)*. With a helper, place the first panel on a couple of bricks or blocks and, after checking for level, pin it temporarily to the inner face of the post *(right)*.

2 Fitting and securing the panels. Adjust the second post in its hole and pin the panel to it. Drive a nail half way into each side of the post, about a third of the way from the top, then brace the post on either side by wedging a support board under each nail. Repeat this procedure until all the panel sections and posts are pinned and braced in place. Fill in the post holes and allow the concrete to set.

Drill three pilot holes through the edges of each panel frame, and attach the panels to the posts with 65 mm galvanized nails or screws. Finally, remove the temporary fixings, the braces and the brick or block supports.

A Special Frame for Louvres

1 Marking a rail. Cut two 100 by 50 mm rails 40 mm longer than the distance between two posts. Draw lines across both rails, at right angles to the long sides, 20 mm in from each end. Stand a scrap of 150 by 25 mm timber diagonally across one rail at the angle you have chosen for the louvres, so that one corner touches the pencil line; trace round its end. Determine the louvre spacing that will produce a good overlap (this is usually 75 to 100 mm) and mark the intervals on one edge of the rail starting from the initial pencil line *(inset)*.

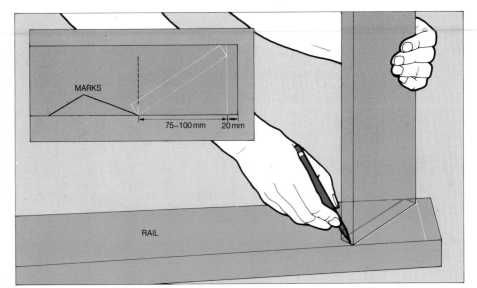

2 Cutting housings with a router and jig. To make a jig, use a sliding bevel to transfer the angle traced on the rail to a piece of scrap timber about 600 mm long. Place two short boards to serve as guides on the marked scrap board at this angle, parallel to each other and separated by the diameter of the router base plate; screw them in place. Lay one of the rails you intend to rout alongside the lower board, then place a second scrap of timber under the guides and against the rail so that the rail will slide between these two lower boards—the crosspieces. Screw the guides to the second crosspiece. Remove the rail.

Fit the router with a straight bit that is equal in diameter to the thickness of your louvres, set it to cut a housing 10 mm deep, and cut 25 mm notches in the crosspieces of the jig by running the router between the two guide boards *(right)*. Clamp the marked rail to a bench and tack the jig to it, carefully aligning the notches in the jig with one of the marks on the rail *(right, below)*. Move the router steadily across the rail; repeat at each mark.

Use this rail as the template to mark the positions of louvres on the second rail and cut housings in it. Partially assemble the louvre panel by slipping two or three 150 by 25 mm boards into position in the housings at each end of the rails and two in the middle; secure them in place by nailing through the rails.

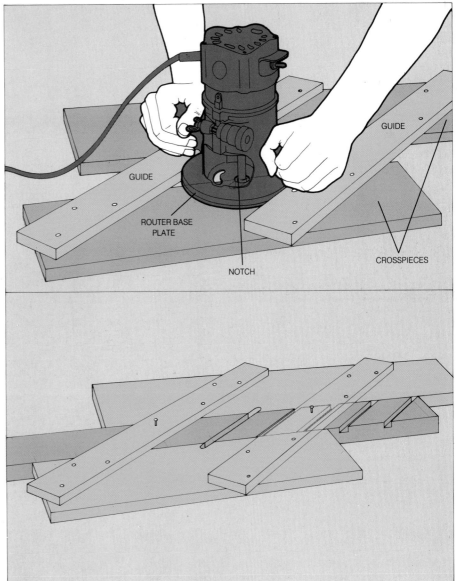

3 **Cutting notches in the posts.** Trace the outline of the rail ends on the inner face of each post, setting the top rail at least 100 mm below the post top to prevent damp from weakening the joint. A water level *(page 8)* will ensure that the marks are perfectly level. Use a marking gauge to outline a notch 20 mm deep at each of these marks. With a handsaw, make parallel cuts 20 mm deep and 10 mm apart across the face of the outline. Set the bevel of a chisel away from you and remove most of the wood inside the outlined notch. Then turn the bevel towards you and neatly finish off the back and sides.

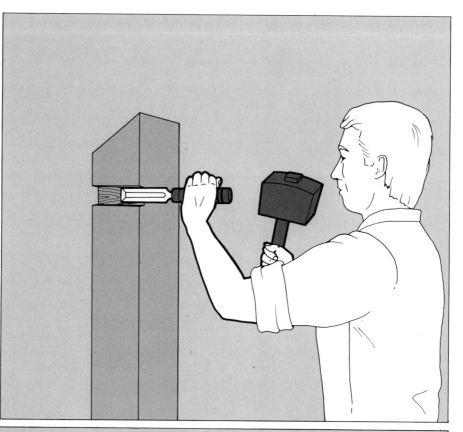

4 **Assembling the fence.** Supporting the bottom rail on blocks, lift the partially assembled louvred panel upright between the posts, slip the rails into the notches and toenail them to the posts. Slip the remaining louvres into their housings, securing them with nails at the top and exterior-grade adhesive at the bottom.

Adapting to Uneven Ground

Building a fence that successfully follows your property's contours often depends on choosing the right style of fence for your land and modifying the design as necessary. A post-and-board fence *(below)* conforms to any terrain and is best for sharply sloping or rolling ground.

On rough but relatively level ground, a fence with vertical pickets or slats *(bottom)* can smooth out small dips and rises; its bot- tom follows the earth's contours while the top remains level. If you plan to build such a fence, buy enough pickets of extra length to fill in the low spots.

Where the ground slopes steadily, one simple solution is to build a fence of vertical boards in a series of steps, following the technique shown on page 50. Uniform stepping requires a few calculations, but once these are done and the posts are in position, attaching rails and boards is straightforward. The fence top can then be levelled off with a circular saw.

As prefabricated panels cannot be tailored to follow the lie of the land, it may be necessary to terrace a slope by digging away or building up the ground along the course of your fence. On land that slopes only slightly, install panels in steps of two or more sections.

Going up and down hills. Set posts on each rise and in each depression and space the remaining posts between them *(page 35)*. For a post-and-board fence like the one on the left, hold or tack the boards in position against the posts and use a combination square to make vertical marks on the boards at the post centres wherever two boards meet. Trim the boards at the marked angles. If you attach slats or pickets to the boards, use a spacer *(page 43, Step 2)* to align them even- ly at a uniform distance above the top board and use a level to plumb them.

Levelling bumps and dips. To line up pickets on uneven ground, hold each one upside down against the rails with its shaped top just off the ground. Mark its bottom end even with the top of the spacer you are using to align all the pickets, and trim at the mark.

Stepping Down a Slope

1 **Fixing posts and rails.** Run a string from ground level at the top of the slope to a tall stake at the bottom and level it with a line or a water level (*page 35*). The height of the string on the tall stake is the vertical drop of the hill. For a long or very steep hill, carry out the procedure by instalments and total the measurements.

By the method using a string plumb bob (*described on page 35*), drive in stakes to mark post locations. Divide the number of fence sections into the total vertical drop to calculate the drop from one section to the next. Set the top end post to the intended fence height, the rest of the posts to the fence height plus the rail drop. Starting from the bottom of the hill, face-nail a top rail to each post, level it and attach it to the adjacent taller post. Fix the bottom rails parallel to the top.

2 **Nailing and trimming the boards.** Choose boards slightly longer than you need and nail them to the rails so that the base of each board follows the slope. Using a circular saw, trim off the boards level with the tops of the posts. Guide your saw with a straightedge batten pinned just below the top of the fence so as to allow for the width of the saw's base plate.

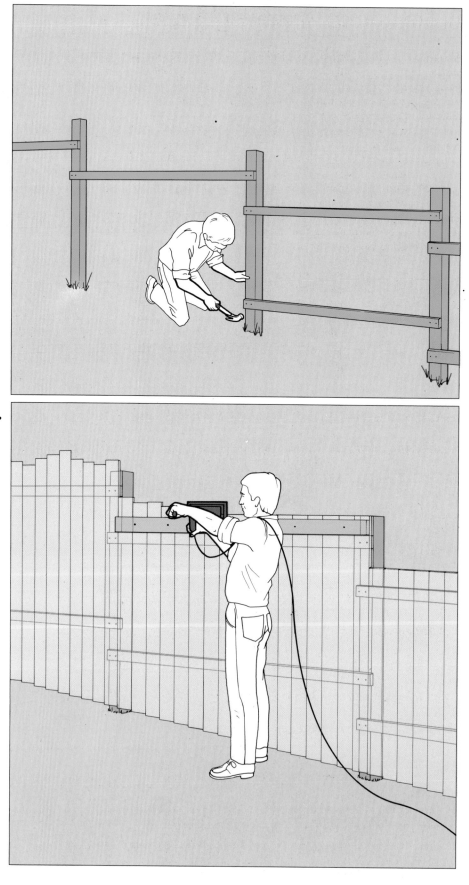

Building and Repairing Gates

A wooden fence gate is often a troublesome object—indeed, the faulty ones sometimes seem to outnumber the good ones. They sag, they bind, they refuse to latch. But, by following three simple precepts, you can have a gate as trouble-free as anyone can reasonably expect.

The first requirement is a pair of strong, plumb gateposts, either set in concrete (*page 37*) or set to a depth equal to one half the height of the part above ground. Space the posts to accommodate the gate width plus a 10 mm clearance for the latch as well as enough clearance for the kind of hinge you plan to install.

The second critical element is a frame that is braced by a diagonal board between the top rail at the latch side and the bottom rail at the hinge side. But no brace can sufficiently stiffen a gate wider than 1500 mm; for a larger opening, install two gates. One gate is held closed with a drop bolt, a 10 mm sliding rod that drops through brackets on the edge of the gate into a hole in the path or driveway; the second gate latches to the first. To provide bottom clearance, hang all gates at least 25 mm above the highest point of ground within the arc of the opening gate.

The third crucial requirement is strong hardware, particularly the hinges (*below*); weak hinges are the most frequent cause of gate problems. To prevent rusting, use black-japanned or galvanized hardware. Among latches, the automatic latch with a thumb lever is a very successful design; sliding bolts are not recommended because even a slight sag in the gate throws them out of alignment.

Even a carefully built gate may eventually sag and bind as its weight pulls hinge screws loose or causes the supporting post to lean. Problems of this nature are relatively easy to correct—leaning posts can be pulled upright again with turnbuckles (*page 53, below*); loose hinge screws can either be tightened up or they can be replaced with longer screws.

For a loose hinge that will not respond to simple first aid, take the gate off the post and, using a twist drill, enlarge the width of the old screw holes and drill the holes to a depth that is three-quarters of the thickness of the post. Cut 10 mm dowels to the depth of the holes, coat them with waterproof glue and tap them into the holes with a mallet. Then drill holes in the dowels, 2 mm smaller than the screws, and rehang the gate. For an inexpensive improvement on this method, replace loose screws with bolts that go completely through the post and are secured by nuts on the other side. However, it is best not to attempt repairs of basic damage, such as rot that severely weakens the wooden parts. It is easier to build a new gate instead.

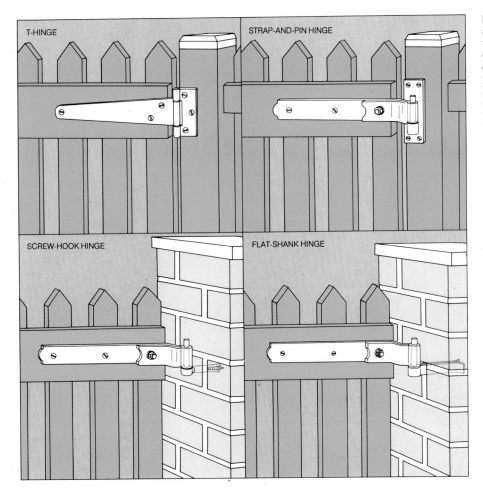

T-HINGE

STRAP-AND-PIN HINGE

SCREW-HOOK HINGE

FLAT-SHANK HINGE

How the hinges go on. These four easily obtainable styles of hinge have one element in common: they all attach to the gate with a strap at least a quarter of the gate's width. A T-hinge (*far left, above*) is connected with a hinge pin to a rectangular plate mounted on the gatepost. A heavy-duty strap-and-pin hinge (*left, above*) comes in two sections—the strap hooks over a vertical pin attached to the post, allowing easy removal of the gate for minor repairs. The strap is often secured to the gate with a coach bolt through the hole nearest the pin.

Hinges mounted on masonry supports are usually secured to the inside face of a wall or pier. The pin of a screw-hook hinge (*far left, below*) is mounted on a horizontal screw which is secured with a plug in the wall. The flat-shank hinge (*left, below*) has a forked flange embedded in a mortar joint during the construction of the wall.

Making and Hanging a Gate

1 Assembling the frame. Cut 100 by 50 mm boards the width of the gate for rails and, using a square to guarantee right angles, position pickets or boards to the rail ends so that the rails of the gate will align with those of the main fence. For a fence 1500 mm or more tall, add a third rail at the middle of the frame. Before you proceed to the next step, nail both of the end pickets to the rails, then turn the frame over.

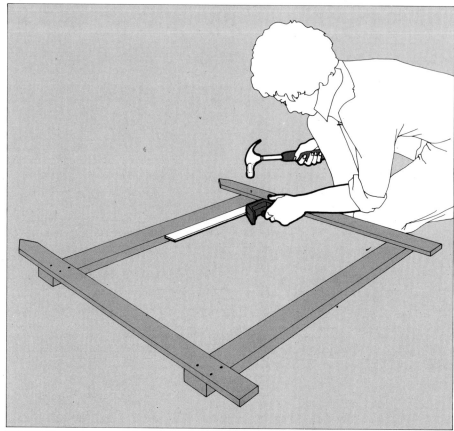

2 Bracing the frame. Mark and cut a 100 by 50 mm brace with angled ends to fit diagonally between the gate's top corner at the latch side and the bottom corner at the hinge side. Secure it with 100 mm wood screws started about 50 mm in from each end and angled into the rails.

Nail the remaining pickets to the rails and the brace. Fasten the hinge straps to the ends of the rails, making sure you leave enough clearance for the hinge to swing easily.

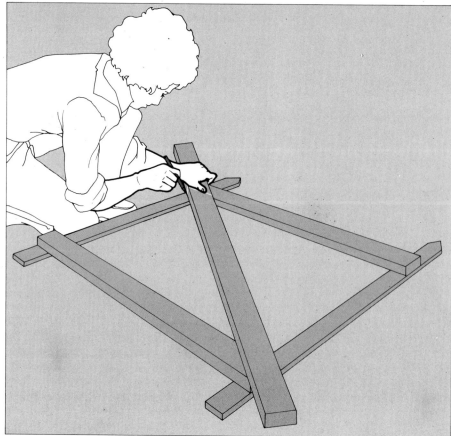

3 **Hanging the gate.** Set the gate on wood scraps to align it with the fence, allowing enough space between the gate frame and the post for the hinge to operate. For a T-hinge *(right)*, mark and drill pilot holes on the post for the mounting plate, then secure the plate with countersunk screws. For a strap-and-pin hinge, slot the pin into the strap, then mark and drill pilot holes and secure the mounting plate to the post. Always mount the top hinge first.

Install a latch bar on the gate and a latch on the post *(inset)*. An automatic thumb lever latch is shown here; most gate latches are installed in the same way. To make a gate stop, nail a strip of 50 by 25 mm timber to the inside face of the latch post. Position it so as to prevent the metal latch bar from taking the full force of the gate when it swings shut.

Remedies for Sags

Plumbing a leaning post. Pull the post to vertical with two 3 mm galvanized wire cables and a turnbuckle fitted with 10 mm eyes. With cable clamps, secure one end of each cable to a 10 mm eyebolt, one at the top of the gatepost and the other at the bottom of the nearest fence post. Similarly, secure the other ends of the cables to the turnbuckle *(inset)*, then tighten the turnbuckle by turning it with a screwdriver.

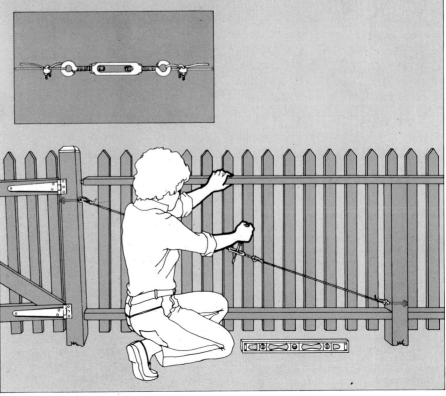

Blocks and Bricks for a Strong High Wall

Masonry walls make the most permanent of all fences, and they are also capable of taking nature's punishment for generations. Yet, for all their sturdiness, they need not be forbidding ramparts. Softened by climbing plants or brightened up by patterns *(pages 61–63)*, even a massive 1800 mm wall of brick or blocks can be a graceful garden ornament in addition to being a property boundary, a windbreak or a guardian of privacy.

A high masonry wall requires care in planning and some skill in its construction if it is to be safely sturdy; an amateur attempting one should first gain experience with the basic masonry techniques. It is large below ground as well as above and must sit on soil that is firm enough to support it; also, it must not block natural drainage. Check drain and cable locations before digging the wall's foundation, and take special care not to violate property lines or local regulations governing setback distances. For a wall that is to be higher than 1 metre, submit a plan to your local building control officer—not only can he tell you of any specific requirements affecting the structure of the wall, but he can advise you on the precise size and depth of the footing, the underground mass of solid concrete that supports the wall.

As a general rule, the base of a concrete footing lies 500 mm or more below ground level. It should be at least 150 mm deep and twice as wide as the wall it supports. At either end of the proposed wall and on either side of piers, the footing should extend a distance equal to half the width of the wall or a minimum of 100 mm. In average soil conditions, the 2 metre wall with piers described on the following pages will require a footing that is 650 mm wide, at least 250 mm deep, and set in a trench approximately 1 metre deep. A trench that is more than a metre deep will generally require shoring up with timber—a job best left to a professional.

For a wall more than 4 or 5 metres long, consider hiring a mini-excavator. These machines are time-saving, but should be used only where there is plenty of space for them to manoeuvre.

Before you begin digging, mark the borders of the footing trench and the centre line of the wall on the ground with a trickle of sand; drive in stakes clear of the digging area, to fix the marks. Allow space for dumping the excavated earth—next to the trench and on your own property. Remember that in loose soil you may have to bank the sides of the trench back from the bed by as much as 45 degrees, in order to keep them from caving in. Keep the bottom of the trench as level and flat as you can, but do not smooth it off by filling loose earth back in: the footing must rest on undisturbed earth. If any virgin soil at the proper depth is loose, remove it and fill the depressions with a "lean" (1 part cement to 12 parts all-in ballast) concrete mix.

In any but the loosest soil, you will not need wooden forms to pour concrete for a footing. In most soils, you should widen the trench on one side to allow sufficient room to smooth the concrete and to lay blocks and mortar from the footing up to the surface. But if the soil is firm enough to keep the trench walls vertical for their full height, you have a convenient but expensive alternative: you can dig the whole trench no wider than the footing and fill it with concrete to a level about 100 mm below the ground *(below, right)*.

Either kind of footing—standard strip or deep strip, as they are respectively called—will require horizontal reinforcement; this will take the form of two lines of 10 mm steel rods laid along the trench. Also, either footing will probably require enough concrete to warrant an order being placed with a ready-mix firm. Explain what you need the concrete for and ask for an appropriate mix. If it is convenient for you to mix your own, use 6 parts all-in ballast to 1 part cement.

When the cement lorry arrives, make sure you have plenty of helpers on hand. Pouring and levelling concrete is heavy work that must be done quickly. A fully loaded cement mixer may crack a drive or rut a lawn. If you cannot bring the lorry close enough to the trench to pour the concrete directly into it, use wheelbarrows with pneumatic tyres to ferry the concrete from the lorry. Once the concrete has been poured and levelled, cover it with plastic sheeting and leave it to cure for 24 hours before starting to build on it.

Preparing a Solid Footing

Two types of deep footing. The trenches on the right contain two types of poured-concrete footing. The first trench, known as a standard strip footing, is suitable for average soils. It has one wall as nearly vertical as the firmness of the soil allows; the bottom is squared off to the width and height of the footing, and above that the trench gets 500 to 600 mm wider, to create a shelf for working space. Reinforcing rods are laid, concrete is poured and levelled, then a block foundation is built to within two brick courses of ground level. The trench on the far right, or deep strip footing, is dug in very firm soil, and has vertical walls separated by the width of the footing. Reinforcement is laid and the trench is almost filled with concrete; it needs no block foundation.

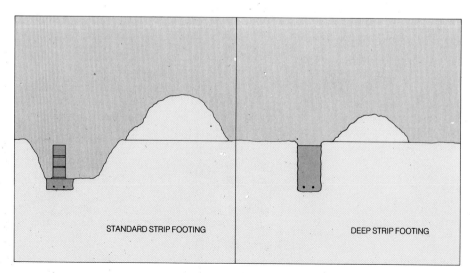

STANDARD STRIP FOOTING

DEEP STRIP FOOTING

Placing the Concrete

1 Levelling the bed. At 1 metre intervals, drive parallel rows of stakes into the ground along each side of the bed of the footing trench. Choose one stake at a high spot in the trench bed, mark it at a point level with the surface of the intended footing; then, using clear plastic tubing and water by the method shown on page 8, mark all the stakes at the same level.

2 Positioning the grade pegs. Next to each stake, drive in a grade peg—a length of reinforcing rod—so that its top is exactly level with the mark on the stake. Be careful not to drive the pegs in too deep. Remove the stakes and tamp the earth round each peg. Check the levels of the pegs with a spirit level taped to a straight length of 100 by 50 mm timber long enough to span three pegs. If a peg is high, tap it lightly to drive it in deeper.

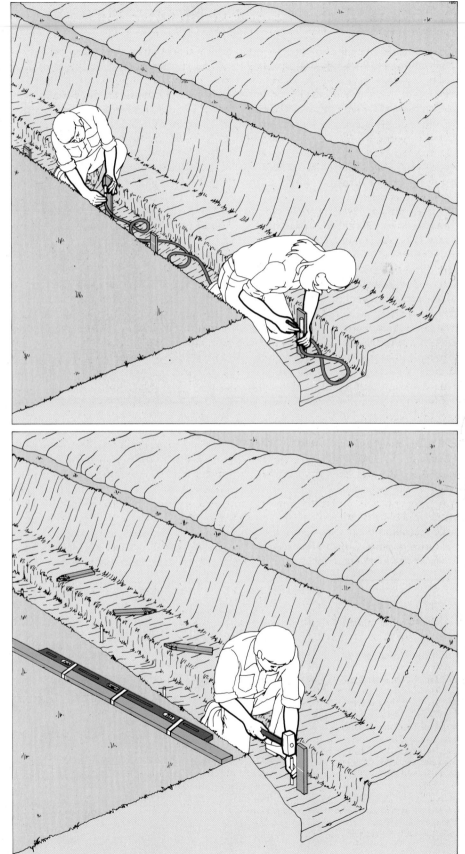

3 **Laying reinforcing rods.** Set lengths of 10 mm reinforcing rod alongside each row of grade pegs and 75 mm in from the ends of the footing, supporting the rods 50 to 75 mm above the trench bed on bricks or stones. Where two bars meet, overlap them for 300 to 400 mm, and use tie wire to lash the overlapping rods to each other and to the grade pegs.

4 **Completing the footing.** Working with helpers, pour concrete into the trench and spread it with square-tipped shovels, digging into it to break up air pockets. When the grade pegs are covered by at least 10 mm of concrete, use a length of 100 by 50 mm timber about 2 metres long as a tamping beam. With a helper at one end, work across the trench, lifting the beam up and down to compact the concrete *(left)*.

After tamping the entire surface, remove any excess concrete above the pegs by dragging the beam across the footing, zigzagging it back and forth as you pull it towards you. Leave the surface rough to provide a key for the mortar. When you finish, the tops of the grade pegs should be barely visible at the surface of the concrete.

Laying Blocks and Bricks

In addition to deep footings, high masonry walls need lateral support. A freestanding garden wall 215 mm thick and more than 1200 mm high should be braced against winds and climbing children. It can be supported with piers—thick columns built into the wall—to give it a broader base, or with vertical steel rods embedded in the footing. The 215 mm wall shown on these pages is reinforced with square piers that are 440 mm on a side.

For any wall, it is most economical to build from the top of the footing up to near ground level with inexpensive concrete blocks. You will need blocks measuring 440 by 215 by 215 mm, together with a few half blocks to avoid having to cut the whole ones; double-ended blocks; and narrow blocks measuring 440 by 215 by 100 mm for the piers. Arrange to have all the blocks delivered on pallets if possible, and keep them dry.

Begin laying bricks two courses below ground level. For a wall like the one on the following pages you will need 120 bricks per square metre, plus two bricks per course per pier. Add another six bricks per pier for any additional pier course above the height of the wall, plus another 28 bricks for each pier capping.

Piers should be spaced 2.5 to 3 metres apart; try to make the total length of the wall and the distance between piers divisible by 225 mm, to facilitate brick-and-block construction. The cores of the blocks in the piers should be filled with concrete—not mortar—from the footing up. Keep in mind that a pier is useful as a wall support only if it is perfectly plumb, which requires scrupulous checking with a level.

You will also need rolls of bituminous felt or plastic damp-proof course to run twice the length of the wall, and enough reinforcing mesh to run the length of the wall every six courses.

1 Aligning the blocks. Snap the two chalk lines along the near side of the footing, the first, half a block's width from the centre, to mark the edge of the bottom course of blocks, and another the same distance outside the first, to mark the edge of the piers. Lay a dry run of the first course to the chalk lines, with a pair of blocks at each pier. Leave a 10 mm space between the ends of the blocks to allow for the mortar joints. Adjust the thickness of the joints to bring the course to the correct length. Mark the location of each pier with chalk on the footing.

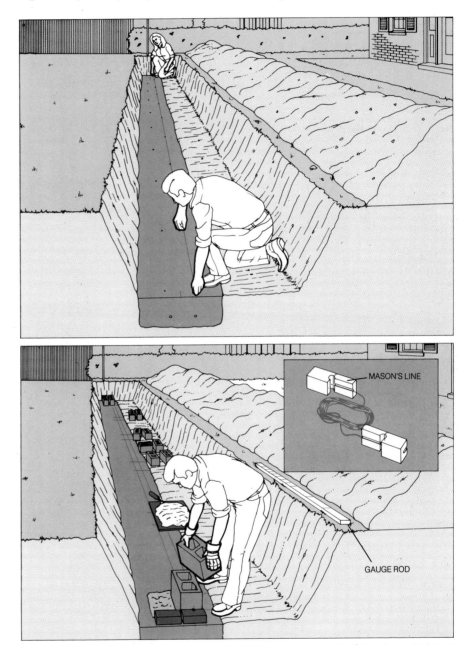

MASON'S LINE

GAUGE ROD

2 First course. At the marks for one of the end piers, lay two double-ended blocks side by side in a full mortar bed. Gauge how much space to leave between the blocks by placing two bricks end to end across the footing, with the end of one brick at the outside chalk line, and 10 mm between the bricks. Lay the blocks so that their outside edges are even with the ends of the bricks. This will leave a small gap between the blocks; the space should be empty. Check both blocks for plumb and level with a spirit level; check the height of their mortar bed with a gauge rod—a home-made measuring stick marked where the top of each course should be when its mortar joint is the right thickness.

Lay two more double-ended blocks for the other end pier, run a mason's line *(inset)* between the two ends and lay pairs of similar blocks for the other piers to the line *(above)*. Fill their cores with concrete.

3 **Completing the first course.** Lay a block in mortar inside each end pier and on both sides of the other piers, centring the blocks on the joint between the two pier blocks—use the inside chalk line as a guide. After the mortar has begun to set, stick two line pins in the vertical joints between the piers and blocks and run a mason's line from one to the other. This establishes a guideline for laying the other blocks between each pair of piers. Fill in the blocks for each section and point up the holes in the mortar left by the line pins.

4 **Completing the foundation.** Begin the second course of blocks with a half block at each end, centred over the joint between the pier blocks. Lay a full-sized block inside each half block, run a mason's line from one end to the other and fill in between them with ordinary blocks. Next, lay blocks measuring 440 by 215 by 100 mm at the end, sandwiching the newly laid second-course blocks as shown below. Three sides of these

narrow blocks must be plumb with the paired double-ended blocks beneath them. Make similar sandwiches at the other piers with the aid of a mason's line run from the ends. For the third course, repeat the first.

When the mortar has set, fill the block cavities at each pier with concrete, to create a continuous column of concrete from the footing up to a few millimetres from the top of the third course.

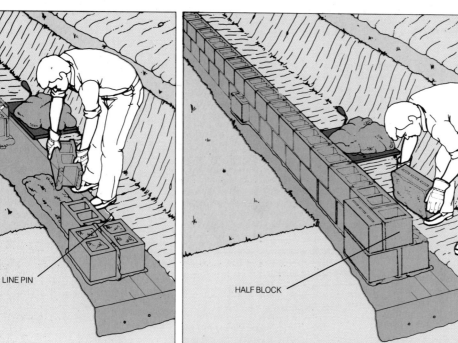

LINE PIN

HALF BLOCK

5 **A dry run.** With the foundation built up almost to ground level, lay a dry run of the first course of bricks, to adjust their fit from pier to pier. Lay the bricks in the pattern shown on the right and set a half block at the core of each pier. The bricks in the piers should be plumb with the blocks beneath them on three sides; keep any overlap on one side as shown. Between piers, separate two rows of bricks so that a brick laid across them fits plumb. Separated in this way, the two rows of bricks should be plumb with the single row of blocks they rest on. If there is any overlap, keep it on the far side of the wall so that the near side can be plumbed up from the foundation.

Make sure that the gaps between bricks are not aligned with the vertical joints below, then mark the position of the bricks on the blocks with chalk and remove the dry run.

OVERLAP

6 **Laying the first bricks.** Spread mortar on the tops of the blocks of an end pier and on 350 mm of the adjoining wall. Starting 25 mm from the pier's end, roll out reinforcing mesh and press it firmly into the mortar. Using the dry-run pattern, lay bricks round the pier rim and one and a half brick lengths out along the wall. Set a half block in the middle of the pier; double-check each brick for level and plumb. Build up the corner to three courses, setting each course one half brick shorter to form steps. The top of the third course should be level with the top of the block set in the pier (*above*). Fill the half block with concrete.

Roll out the mesh along the length of the wall on a 5 mm bed of mortar. Work in 2 metre stages so that the mortar has not set before the mesh is in place. At the end pier, build another three-course corner. Build the intermediate piers to the same height as the end piers but with the steps of bricks extending out along the wall at both sides. Use a mason's line strung from the end piers to maintain alignment. Run a line from pins stuck in the vertical mortar joints next to the piers and, checking repeatedly for level and plumb, build up the wall to three courses between the piers.

7 **Installing the first damp-proof course.** Cut two short strips of damp-proof course to lie side by side over the tops of each pier, and bed them in 3 to 5 mm of mortar. Starting at one end pier, spread a thin layer of mortar for 2 metres along the top of the wall, then roll out the damp-proof course, pressing it into the mortar with a brick or trowel. Work along the wall in 2 metre lengths, overlapping the damp-proof course on the end piers by at least 100 mm.

8 **Extending the wall upwards.** From the first damp-proof course, build up the end and middle piers three more courses, as described on page 59, Step 6. On both sides of the footing, fill in the trench with soil and compact it thoroughly. Lay another layer of reinforcing mesh on top of the sixth complete course. From this height, build the wall upwards in six-course stages. The lower steps of the piers will now run three and a half brick lengths along the wall *(below)*. Build in reinforcing mesh every six courses. Twenty brick courses will take the wall up to a height of 1500 mm above the block footings, 24 brick courses will take it to 1800 mm.

9 **Finishing the wall.** When the wall is two courses short of the height you want, lay a second damp-proof course *(page 59, Step 7)* followed by another course of bricks. Install a final layer of reinforcing mesh and build up the piers another three courses. Lay a brick-on-edge coping on the mesh, starting with a dry run and adjusting the joints as necessary for a proper fit.

10 **Capping the piers.** For each pier, cut eight 30 mm thick pieces of brick (that is, pieces measuring 30 by 65 by 102.5 mm), called closers, to use in widening the cap courses. Following the basic pier pattern, lay the first course of the cap with full-sized bricks—known as oversailors—round the rim of the pier so that they project 20 mm over the edge on all sides. Fit four of the closer pieces between the whole bricks, one on each side, to fill out the course. Set two bricks in the middle of the pier and fill all the space round them with mortar.

Alternating the pattern, lay the second oversailor course plumb with the first. Put two more bricks in the centre and grout solid with mortar. For the final course, lay a double brick-on-edge cap centred on the pier.

Spread a thick bead of mortar at the base of the double brick-on-edge course, and smooth it with a trowel to a 45-degree fillet.

MORTAR FILLET

Decorative Masonry Patterns

Masonry walls need not always present a solid, unvarying face. Bricks and blocks can be laid in different patterns to enliven a wall's appearance, and in open designs to admit light and air while at the same time screening a view.

Decorative patterns for walls made of blocks, particularly those with openings, most often use a form of stacked bond: the units do not overlap but have their vertical joints lined up. The lack of overlapping joints weakens the wall, which therefore requires strengthening with mesh and steel rods (right, above). Horizontal joint reinforcement should be embedded in the mortar along the full length of the wall after every second or third course of blocks—after each course with 300 mm screen blocks. Where the hollow cores of blocks align vertically, reinforcing bars at 1200 mm intervals should be run from the footing up through the blocks at least half way up the wall.

The block patterns illustrated on page 62 use stacked bond and blocks of widely available, standard sizes. Odd sizes give you more complex patterns but, whatever pattern you choose, arrange blocks so that continuous reinforcement can be laid between courses and so that very few blocks stand on end, the position in which they weaken the wall most.

Bricks can also be used to make openwork, but such walls require a skilled bricklayer in order to make them structurally sound. An amateur bricklayer, however, can build a solid brick wall with a decorative pattern based on the interplay of headers (bricks laid crosswise on the wall) and stretchers (bricks laid along the length of the wall). Such decorative designs strengthen an ordinary "one-brick" garden wall—that is, a wall that is equal in thickness to the length of a brick—since the headers tie the front and back courses of brick together, performing part of the function of joint reinforcement.

Most of the traditional brick patterns are developed either from English bond, in which courses of headers and stretchers alternate (right, centre), or from Flemish bond, which has alternating headers and stretchers in each course (right, below). Variations of these two basic bonds will produce an enormously varied range of ornamental patterns, which can be heightened still further by using bricks of contrasting colours.

A large brickyard will stock from 20 to 30 different colours of brick; however, for a simple design such as those illustrated, you need only two colours of standard-faced building brick, one for a background and the other for the pattern. Buy all the bricks you require at the same time: colours vary considerably from batch to batch, and you may not be able to match bricks later.

To determine how many bricks you need in each colour, draw a diagram on graph paper of the pattern you plan to use. Make each course one square high; let two horizontal squares represent a header and four squares a stretcher. Include enough complete courses (usually two or three) to show the bond pattern, count the number of odd-coloured bricks in these courses and multiply the figure by the number of pattern repeats you will need for the entire wall. Double the number of odd-coloured stretchers if you want the pattern to show on both sides of a wall two courses thick; add the odd-coloured headers and subtract the total from the number of bricks needed for the whole wall (page 57). Also, you should buy 5 per cent extra in both colours, to allow for any breakages.

When you design a wall with one of the pattern units shown in the centre and far right rows on page 63, you must design it from the centre to make the pattern symmetrical, although you will actually build the wall from its ends. On graph paper, draw an outline of a full section of the wall. Make the wall an odd number of courses high—the course that serves as a horizontal axis for the design must have an even number of courses above and below it. Find the squares that represent the centre brick of the section. Fill in the pattern unit over this centre brick, then fill in the rest of the section. You can now tell how many pattern units or parts of units will fit into the section and the wall, and how to begin laying the bricks.

The diagram will also show that, to make a design with Flemish bond or English bond, alternate courses must include a quarter brick—known as a "queen closer" (right)—which is placed next to the corner header at either end of the wall. Queen closers are necessary to ensure that vertical joints do not fall above each other.

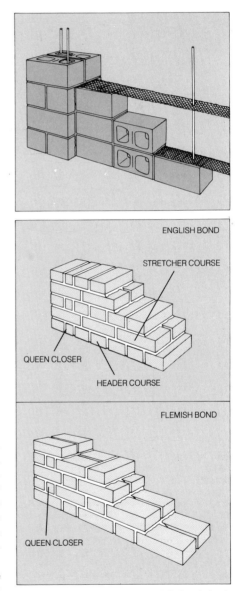

Reinforcing stacked blocks. Walls of stacked bond need both horizontal and vertical reinforcement. The piers bracing the wall below are cross pairs of double-ended blocks, knitted to the rest of the wall with continuous stretchers of joint reinforcement mesh laid after every second course. Steel rods 10 mm in diameter run up through the cores of the blocks of each pier and at 1200 mm intervals between piers. The cores with the rods are filled with concrete.

ENGLISH BOND

STRETCHER COURSE

QUEEN CLOSER

HEADER COURSE

FLEMISH BOND

QUEEN CLOSER

Basic ornamental bonds. In English bond (top), header and stretcher courses alternate; in Flemish bond (above), each course consists of alternating header and stretcher bricks. Quarter bricks, or queen closers, are used near the ends of courses to align the headers and stretchers in every other course.

Open and Shut Designs with Blocks

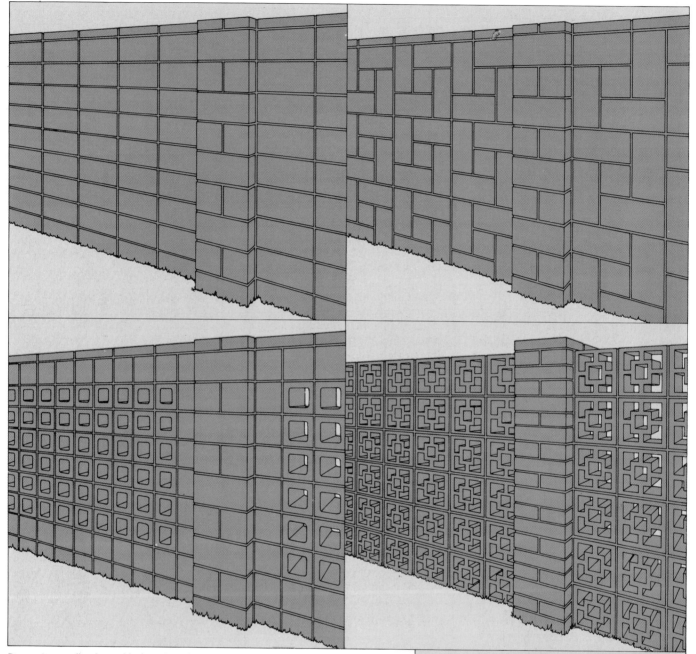

Decorative walls from blocks. Ordinary stretcher blocks in stacked bond *(top, left)* make a surprisingly good-looking wall. A basketweave pattern *(top, right)* is made from units of four stretchers and a half block. More half blocks laid on their sides *(above, left)* can be arranged in a wide variety of patterns to form openings for light and air. Ornamental 300 mm screen blocks *(above, right)* require 100 mm blocks for piers so that horizontal reinforcement can be laid on top of each course. The walls and piers can be capped either with flat, solid blocks *(above)* or with coping stones *(right)* which come in various shapes and overhang the wall on either side.

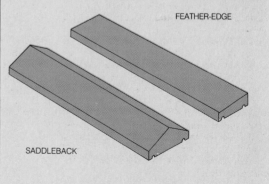

FEATHER-EDGE

SADDLEBACK

Fancy Tricks with Coloured Bricks

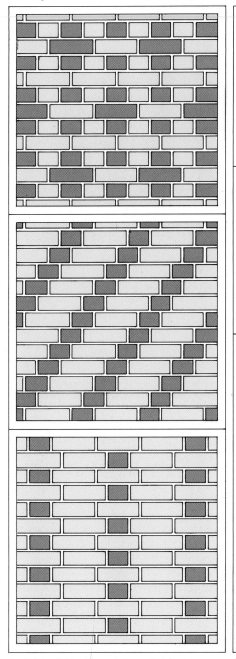

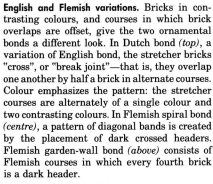

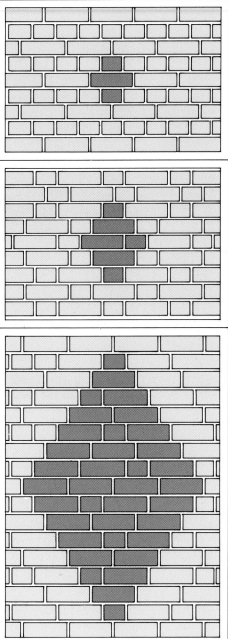

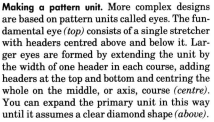

English and Flemish variations. Bricks in contrasting colours, and courses in which brick overlaps are offset, give the two ornamental bonds a different look. In Dutch bond *(top)*, a variation of English bond, the stretcher bricks "cross", or "break joint"—that is, they overlap one another by half a brick in alternate courses. Colour emphasizes the pattern: the stretcher courses are alternately of a single colour and two contrasting colours. In Flemish spiral bond *(centre)*, a pattern of diagonal bands is created by the placement of dark crossed headers. Flemish garden-wall bond *(above)* consists of Flemish courses in which every fourth brick is a dark header.

Making a pattern unit. More complex designs are based on pattern units called eyes. The fundamental eye *(top)* consists of a single stretcher with headers centred above and below it. Larger eyes are formed by extending the unit by the width of one header in each course, adding headers at the top and bottom and centring the whole on the middle, or axis, course *(centre)*. You can expand the primary unit in this way until it assumes a clear diamond shape *(above)*.

Combining pattern units. Large wall designs consist of a number of pattern units defined by coloured bricks and arranged to cover the wall symmetrically. In one widely used design *(top)*, the eyes butt one another, forming horizontal bands, and the bands are emphasized by a course of solid-colour stretchers between the rows of eyes. Coloured borders can make a simple pattern unit into a more complex design: in the example above, each unit is bordered by dark headers.

A Thin, Yet Sinuously Solid Wall

Grace in brickwork. An 1887 drawing depicts an alley on the University of Virginia campus leading to a colonnade and bordered by two of Jefferson's winding walls. An inset shows Jefferson's plan for a series of gardens surrounded by serpentine walls.

To the sharp, enquiring eye of Thomas Jefferson, the graceful serpentine walls that he viewed on a tour of famous English gardens in the late 1780s were both alluring and ingenious. Jefferson was attracted not only to the obvious beauty of the walls—called "crinkle-crankle" in England—but also to their subtle economy. Unlike traditional brick walls, the serpentine design needed no buttressing piers and no double layer of bricks, instead deriving its strength from its built-in curves.

Jefferson saw the serpentine wall as a delightful addition to his plan to blend Old World forms into the grounds of the University of Virginia, and to create a neoclassical "Academical Village" embowered by gardens. In England, he wrote, plants thrived at the bases of serpentine walls, because the walls' curves focused the sun's warmth. Their rippling shadows pleased the eye of the late-afternoon stroller.

To Jefferson's pragmatic mind—he kept track of the budget for the construction of the university, and paid special attention to the price of brick, which he found to be "exorbitant"—the economy of serpentine walls was as important as their aesthetic value. He calculated that, although a serpentine wall was longer than a straight one spanning the same distance, it required only about two-thirds the number of bricks.

The serpentine design is as useful and economical now as it was in the 18th century. It consists of a series of identical curves in a wave-like pattern. The trick now, as then, is to make the height of the wall consistent with the degree of curvature. As the British bricklayers whose work Jefferson admired had discovered, the higher the wall, the more it had to undulate to maintain itself. A low wall could be built in a series of shallow curves; for a higher wall, the curves had to be tighter and needed to extend farther out from the wall's centre line.

Modern bricklayers have reduced these considerations to two handy rules of thumb: the radius of the curves should be less than twice the proposed height of the wall, and the total width of the wall should be more than half the wall's proposed height.

Thus, a serpentine wall with a height of 1200 mm above ground level would have to be built in curves that had a radius of 2400 mm or less and a total width of at least 600 mm. In some parts of the country where high winds prevail, local building regulations might require a wall to be built with tighter curves.

Turning a corner is a simple matter; as the bricklayer arrives at the corner, he continues the curve on which he is working until the corner is turned, then continues his pattern in the new direction.

Ironically, Jefferson's own serpentine walls did not stand. In the 1800s, university administrators complained that the walls were in constant need of repair, and by the turn of the century hardly any were still standing. In 1949, the Garden Club of Virginia undertook the reconstruction of the walls. Following the old ground plans, landscape architects working on the project located some of the original foundations, and were able to rebuild all the serpentine walls exactly where Jefferson had planned them.

But the architects were unable to explain why the original walls had fallen down. They guessed that the bricklayers had not mixed enough crushed oyster shells, a source of lime, into the mortar.

Putting In Metal Railings

Ornamental "iron" railings—which today are steel or aluminium—are among the strongest and most durable of open fences. They also tend to be among the most costly. New ones are generally custom-made at small ironworks and engineering companies, though less expensive prefabricated panels of aluminium or steel bars are available from some retail fence dealers in a limited range of sizes and styles. Many companies now specialize in reproducing Victorian-style railings with a wide selection of ornate railing heads to cap the vertical bars.

Installing new metal railings yourself will save 20 to 30 per cent of the cost of those professionally installed. To order custom-built railings, first consult the ironworks, and then draw up a detailed profile of the railings and the terrain they are to cover. Precise measurements are essential: once the panels are assembled and welded, there is little room for adjustment. The profile *(right, above)* should show the exact contour of the land and the key dimensions of the railings. If the ground is uneven, decide at this stage whether to level it or to have the railings follow the contours, either in steps *(page 50)* or by sloping the horizontal rails.

Ask the ironworks to coat the railings with red oxide or zinc chromate primer before delivery. Before you put them up, give them two coats of oil-based exterior paint.

Making the profile. Run a level string along the line of the railings. Measure the height of the string at the locations of the posts and of significant dips and rises in the ground. Record the profile of the terrain on graph paper and draw in the posts and panels to scale.

Note on the profile the height and length of panels and gates, the spacing and dimensions of the vertical bars and rails, the thickness and total height of the posts (as much as one-third must go below ground in concrete—page 34), the location of the lugs for bolting the panels to the posts, the locations of hinges and latches, and any additional ornamentation. For stepped or sloped railings, note the size of the rail drop *(page 50)* or the angle of the rail slope.

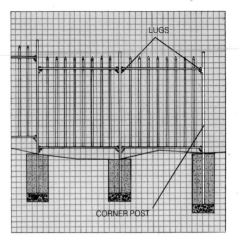

Setting the posts and panels. Because of the precise tolerances of metal railings, posts are put up together with panels, and the assembled units are plumbed and braced in position in the post holes. When the railings are delivered, dig post holes and put 100 to 150 mm of coarse gravel in each hole. Run a low string precisely along the line of the railings. Start at an end, corner or gate, bolt posts to both sides of a panel and mark the posts with chalk to show how much should be set above ground level.

Place both posts, with the panel in place between them, in their holes just inside the string, supporting the panel with blocks under the bottom rail. Adjust the gravel in the holes until it supports the posts at the correct height and the panel is level or properly sloped. Plumb each post and brace the panel from both sides with notched 100 by 50 mm supports nailed to stakes.

Bolt a third post to the next panel and attach the free end to the braced panel. Level, plumb and brace as before, repeating the procedure until all the panels are up and secure. At gates, set and brace a gatepost and panel on one side of a gate opening, then mount the gate to locate the other gatepost and panel. Before filling the holes with concrete *(page 37)*, check once more to see that all posts are plumb and aligned.

65

Ready for installation. Materials suitable for covering the roofs and walls of light outdoor structures range from rolls of woven reed and lengths of bamboo to plastic or wire mesh and a crisscrossing framework of wooden lattice. Designed for openness, these materials are so light in weight that in most cases all you need for fastening them to a structure is an ordinary staple gun.

Like Kubla Khan decreeing a stately pleasure dome, you can embellish your garden Xanadu with a truly spectacular dome—or with a shed, a pergola, a tree house or a gazebo. But unlike the subject of Coleridge's famous poem, you can carry out the decree personally and build the structure yourself. Moreover, you can build it with a minimum of time, labour and expense since, unlike the great Khan, you have available an astonishing variety of techniques. They make possible structures that, while not built for the ages, are sturdy enough to last for as long as you will want to use them.

Of the many methods available for building the structures shown on the following pages, some, like the post-and-beam, are older than the pyramids; others, like the geodesic dome, are recent adaptations of ancient forms. But, for all of them, you begin by erecting a skeleton. To build an A-frame, for example, you first erect inverted Vs of jointed timbers to serve as ribs of the combination roof-walls. Similarly, with post-and-beam buildings, you first raise the posts and then link them with horizontal beams. This technique—which man developed for his first wooden dwellings, refined for the Parthenon and still uses for skyscrapers—is strong, yet leaves large open spaces between the supports.

A structural skeleton on its own may be enough for a pergola, but to provide shade you may want to add a partial covering, and for a storage shed you need to provide a weatherproof skin. Sheathing and cladding materials for roofs and walls often do double duty: traditional wood, chipboard and plywood combine sheathing with weatherproofing. Decorative lattice, bamboo and woven-reed coverings also moderate the glare of sun and the blast of wind. Inexpensive plastic panels repel wind and water but admit light.

When you imaginatively combine decorative sheathings with fanciful frames, the whole structure becomes fun. The gazebo, a multi-sided post-and-beam structure, lends itself to the addition of lattices, curlicues and cupolas. As for tree houses, only the fertile imagination of youth is needed to convert an arboreal platform into a castle, a spaceship or a frigate's quarterdeck.

One type of lightweight structure is not an offspring of traditional construction methods at all, but the brainchild of a 20th-century genius who worked out how to weave a web of triangles into the shape of the age-old hemispherical dome. Buckminster Fuller's geodesic domes are based on the geometric shape called an icosahedron. And yet, advanced mathematics plays no great role in dome-building—you can erect this lacing of struts as easily as you can erect a square shed, and people will admire your many-faceted pleasure dome even if they have never heard of its technical name.

The A-Frame: a Modern Tent Built with Plywood

One of the simplest of all buildings takes the form of a braced triangle—an A-frame—rising from the ground. Nailed together at the peak of an A-frame, the rafters that serve as both roof and walls enclose a structure that is practical for many types of small outdoor building. A low A-frame, with a peak 1 to 1.5 metres above the ground, might be used as a pet shelter or a storage shed; a higher one, with 1.8 metres or more of headroom, can serve as a garden house or a playroom.

In every A-frame, the walls that form the roof are equal, but the angle at the peak may vary considerably, and this angle affects both headroom and floor space. A typical A-frame, like the one on these pages, is an equilateral triangle,

with a base and sides of exactly the same length. A-frames with steeper sides have more headroom, but proportionately less floor space; flattening the triangle has the opposite effect.

Before you begin any building, make a scale drawing of the A-frame in order to measure the slope, or pitch, of the roof. This is expressed in degrees and determines the angles at which rafters are cut at top and bottom. Mark rafters for cutting with a pitchboard—a right-angled triangle of plywood or hardboard with one angle equalling the degree of pitch (page 70, Step 2). The A-frame on these pages has a pitch of 60 degrees.

The rafters of an A-frame, like those of any two-sided roof, must be reinforced to

prevent them spreading and sagging. In a small A-frame that rests directly on the ground or on a bed of gravel, you can brace the rafters with cross ties (called collar beams). In structures where headroom is valued, the horizontal reinforcements can be built into the floor. If you intend to use your A-frame for storage alone, simply bolt the rafters to a reinforced concrete slab (below). In garden shelters or playhouses, sandwich the rafters between wooden joists (opposite page, above), and install flooring (pages 98–99).

Whatever the size of your A-frame, the lower ends of rafters must be secured to timber sole plates. Coat these thoroughly with bitumen-based paint, in order to protect the wood from damp.

A Compact, Triangular Structure

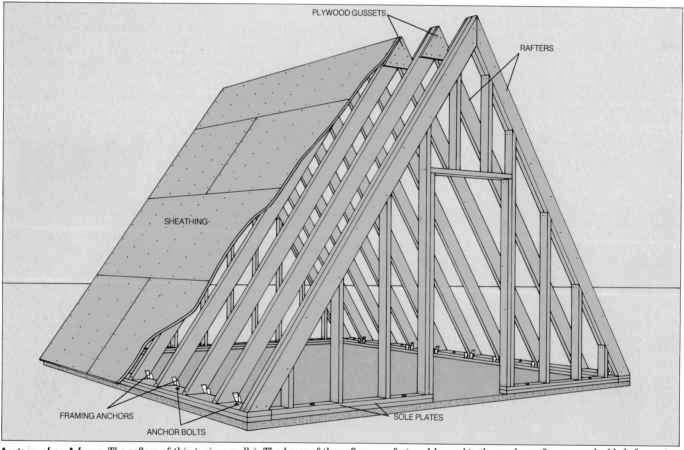

Anatomy of an A-frame. The rafters of this typical A-frame are 150 by 50 mm boards, joined at their peaks with triangular plywood gussets (the gussets on the outermost rafters are omitted so that sheathing will lie flat against the vertical walls). The bases of the rafters are fastened by metal framing anchors, and the doubled sole plates are fixed to a concrete slab with anchor bolts. The sole plates along the sides of the A-frame pictured here are 225 by 50 mm boards. At the ends, rafters are doubled for extra strength; they enclose a framework of studs which are toenailed to 100 by 50 mm sole plates. The entire structure is covered with exterior-grade plywood or pre-felted chipboard.

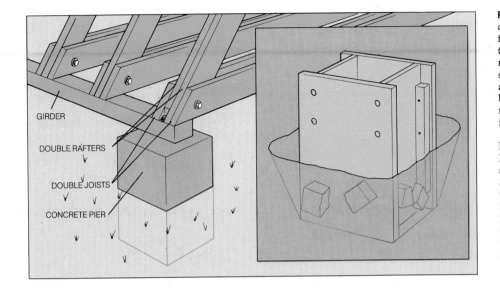

GIRDER

DOUBLE RAFTERS

DOUBLE JOISTS

CONCRETE PIER

Piers for a wooden floor. Concrete piers serve as a foundation for an A-frame with a wooden floor. The 100 by 100 mm timber girders pictured here are adequate for spans of up to 1.5 metres; they are secured to the piers with bolts set in expanding anchors *(page 75, Step 1)*. Joists and rafters are fastened together with 16 mm bolts and then toenailed to the girders. (Where a rafter falls on a girder bolt, chisel a triangle off its end to clear the bolt head.)

To make a concrete pier, dig a flat-bottomed hole 300 mm deep and about 500 mm square. Into this, place a wooden form *(inset)* 300 mm square and 600 mm high, secured with screws above ground level. For extra strength, overlap two opposite sides and nail 50 by 25 mm battens into the external corners. Wedge stones or brick fragments round the form, coat the inner surfaces with oil and fill the form with a foundation mix *(Step 1, below)*. Leave the formwork in place for 24 hours, to allow the concrete to set.

Laying the Foundation

REINFORCING MESH

FORM BOARDS

1 Preparing the slab. Clear topsoil from the foundation area and build a rectangular wooden form of 150 by 25 mm boards supported by stakes. Lay a 50 mm sub-base of hoggin or crushed stone, filling any gaps with a 25 mm layer of sand. Spread overlapping sheets of 1000-gauge polythene up to the edges of the form, then pour a 25 mm layer of foundation mix—1 part cement to 5 parts all-in ballast. Cover this immediately with 6 mm 200 by 200 mm reinforcing mesh and pour in the remaining concrete, using a mortar hoe or rake to pack each load up against the preceding one until the level is just above the top of the form *(left)*. Thoroughly compact and level the concrete with the edge of a 150 by 50 mm tamping beam.

2 Placing anchor bolts. When the concrete begins to harden, embed 200 mm anchor bolts along the edges of the slab, leaving the top 100 mm of each bolt exposed above the concrete. Run a string along the sides of the slab, half the width of the sole plate in from the edge, and place the first bolt along the string, starting 200 mm from one end; place the remaining bolts at 800 mm intervals. On the front and back of the slab, place the first and last bolts 600 mm from the ends, the remaining ones at 800 mm intervals, half the width of the sole plate in from the edges, but leave a gap in the front row for a door.

Building Roofs That Are Walls

1 **Marking the sides.** On each side of the slab, lay a 225 by 50 mm sole plate against the anchor bolts and, using a combination square, transfer the positions of the bolts to the plate. To centre the bolt-hole locations on the plate, measure the distance from the bolts to the edge of the slab and mark this distance off on the plate.

Mark the rafter locations on the plate between the bolt marks, setting the spacing for 400 mm centres and allowing for double rafters at both ends. Finally, set the plate on a second 200 by 50 mm board cut to the same length, drill through both plates at the positions marked for anchor bolts and bolt the doubled sole plate in place on the slab.

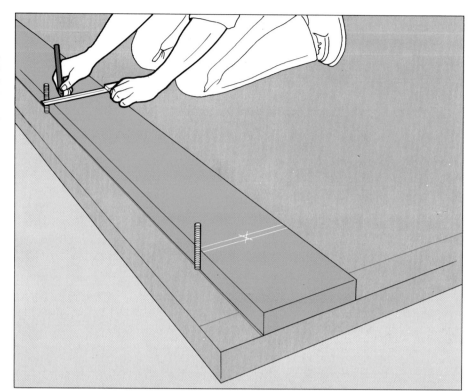

2 **Marking angle cuts.** Make a triangular pitchboard from a square-cornered scrap of 6 mm plywood. Measure from the corner along one edge about 300 mm, then, using a protractor, draw a line at an angle equal to the pitch of the roof— here 60 degrees—to form a right-angled triangle. Cut along this line, and lay the pitchboard across one end of a rafter so that its long side is flush with the lower edge of the board and the angle of pitch is to the right. Draw a line along the left edge of the pitchboard to mark the cut for the rafter peak *(right)*. To mark the cut for the rafter base, move the pitchboard down the rafter until its right-hand corner meets the edge of the board at a point corresponding to the length of the A-frame side. Draw a line along the right edge of the pitchboard *(inset)*.

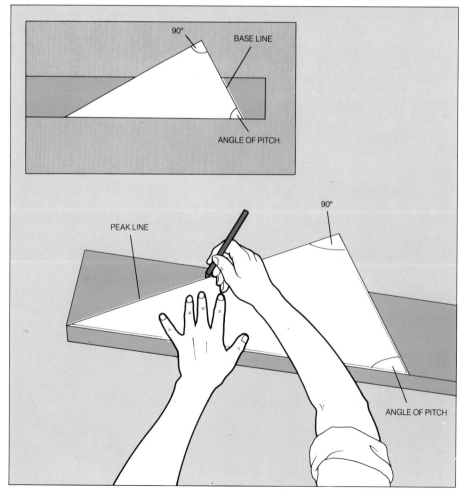

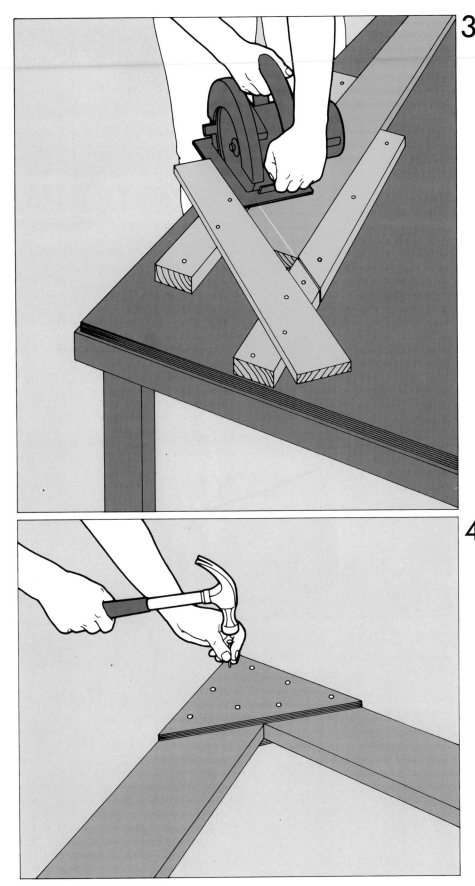

3 **Using a jig.** Saw the rafter-board ends with a circular saw in a home-made cutting jig consisting of two brackets and a guide fence. To make the jig, nail two lengths of 75 by 50 mm timber—the brackets—to a board, spacing them the exact width of a rafter apart. Slip the marked rafter board between the brackets and nail a 100 by 25 mm fence to them, at an angle that matches the angle cut you have marked for the top of the rafter. Check to be sure that the blade of the saw cuts along the rafter mark.

Use the jig to cut the bases of the rafter boards by realigning the fence to match the angle you have cut for the rafter base.

4 **A-joints.** Set pairs of rafters together on the ground to form roof peaks, and nail triangular plywood gussets on both sides of the peak joints, using exterior-grade 12 mm plywood cut to the same angle as the peak. Drive in at least six 50 mm annular nails in a triangular pattern to make the joint secure. Caution: do not nail gussets to the outsides of the front and back peaks.

5 **Setting the first A.** With a helper, raise a pair of double rafters into position over the marked locations at the ends of the sole plates. Brace the rafters temporarily with a scrap 100 by 50 mm timber nailed to a stake about 1500 mm from the slab. Use a spirit level to make sure that the rafters are plumb.

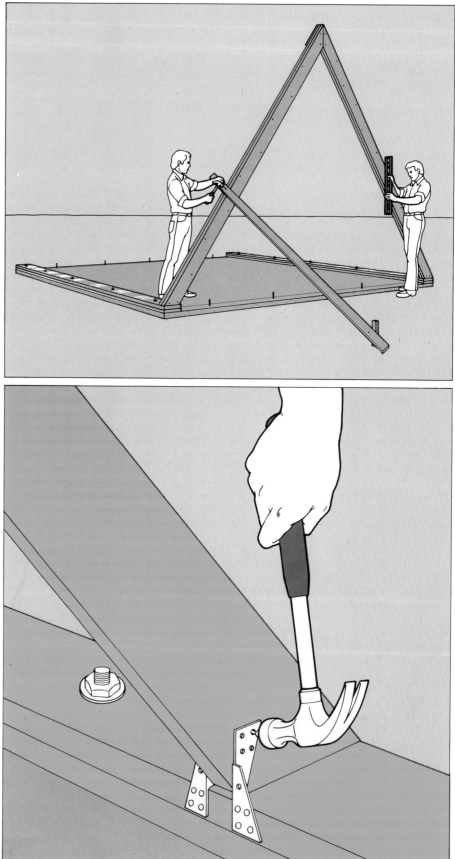

6 **Attaching the framing anchors.** Fasten rafters to the sole plates with metal framing anchors, fastened to both sides of a rafter with 40 mm nails; for additional stability, toenail two 75 mm nails through the outside edge of the rafter into the sole plate. When you have anchored and plumbed three sets of rafters, install temporary stiffeners—horizontal 50 by 25 mm battens nailed into the rafter edges—to keep them steady.

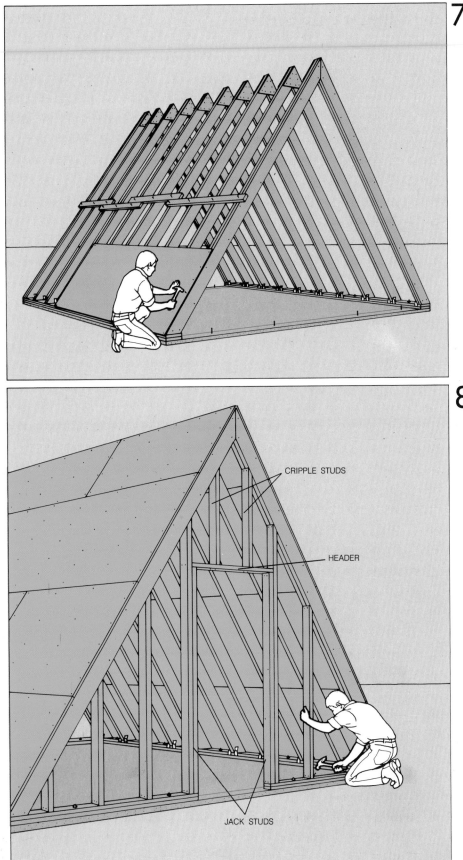

7 **Sheathing the rafters.** Nail 2440 by 1220 mm panels of 12 mm exterior-grade plywood or prefelted chipboard horizontally along the rafters. Begin at the outer edge and bottom of the first rafter. Nail the corners of a panel first, then nail through all the rafters beneath, spacing the nails 150 mm apart. After you have completed the bottom row of sheathing, remove the temporary stiffening and complete the rest of the side. Stagger the joints between panels by cutting the first panel of the second row to end at the midpoint of the panel below. Seal the joints with mastic.

8 **Studding the end walls.** Bolt doubled 100 by 50 mm sole plates to the anchor bolts at the front and back ends of the slab, then install studs for the front and back walls at 400 mm centres, toenailing each stud to the sole plate below and the rafter above. Leave a space for a door in the studding of the front wall; frame the space with jack studs, a header and cripple studs in the front wall. Saw off the sole plates in the door opening and sheathe the ends of the A-frame.

CRIPPLE STUDS

HEADER

JACK STUDS

Post-and-Beam: an Old Method Resurrected

As home owners spend more time in their gardens—and desire structures that make their property more enjoyable—they are discovering the advantages of post-and-beam construction. For the supporting framework this type of construction uses a few big pieces of timber, widely spaced, instead of the many closely spaced 100 by 50 mm studs, stiffened with sheathing, normally associated with modern timber-frame housing. The post-and-beam construction method, which is rarely used nowadays for house building, is particularly adapted for outdoor uses.

To construct a post-and-beam framework, you anchor two parallel rows of wooden posts, connect the posts in each row with crossbeams to form a wall and then tie the walls together with rafters. Left as is, the post-and-beam framework can be used as a pergola or a trellis; roofed and sheathed with any of a variety of openwork materials (pages 92–97), it becomes a breezy garden shelter. With weatherproof sheathing and roofing, the structure can be a workshop, shed, studio or garage.

The intended purpose determines the foundation of a post-and-beam building.

For an open-roofed structure, a simple concrete slab or set of pre-cast concrete piers is adequate (page 69). A closed-roofed structure, particularly one that is to be used as a garage, should have a reinforced raft foundation (pages 104–109) or concrete footings (pages 54–56).

The size of the posts for an unroofed structure is determined by the width of the structure—the distance between the two walls. If the width is less than 2.5 metres, 75 by 75 mm posts will suffice; for a span that is between 2.5 and 3.5 metres, use posts 100 mm square. A roofed structure that is up to 3.5 metres wide also requires posts 100 mm square.

A beam must be the same thickness as the posts it rests upon; its depth depends upon the span between posts along the side of the structure. Use timber 150 mm deep for spans up to 2 metres, and 225 mm deep for spans up to 3 metres.

Rafters are generally 50 mm thick. To calculate their depth, divide the distance in millimetres across the width of the structure by 20, add 20 to the result, and then choose the nearest standard-sized timber to this figure. For example, a 3-metre span

would require a 175 by 50 mm rafter (3000 mm divided by 20 equals 150; plus 20 equals 170). For an open-roofed structure, the spacing between rafters can be anything from 400 to 750 mm, but for a closed roof, never more than 450 mm.

There are several different methods of anchoring posts to concrete. The square post shoe, available from builders' merchants, is one popular solution. Bolt its base plate to your concrete slab, then slot a post into the box-shaped socket. The more sophisticated post shoe shown on the opposite page has a raised support to protect the timber from damp; it is equipped with an offset washer, which allows for a final adjustment to the post's position.

Engineering workshops will make up post shoes to your specifications for any size of timber. It is not difficult, however, to make your own post shoes by cutting strips of galvanized steel, 3 to 4 mm thick, and bending them into a U-shape to fit the base of your posts. Drill nail holes through both sides and two bolt holes in opposite corners of the base. Whatever form of post shoe you use, make sure the post is plumb before finally tightening the bolt.

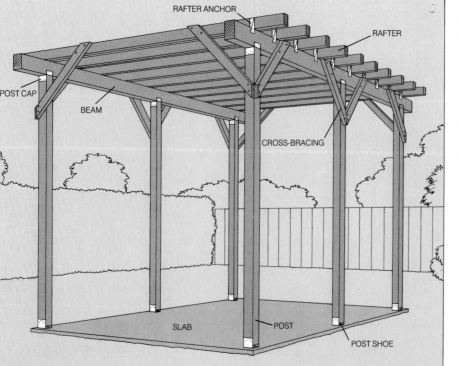

Anatomy of post-and-beam. Metal anchors hold together the basic post-and-beam framework. The posts are attached to post shoes fastened in a concrete slab *(left)*, or to pre-cast concrete piers *(page 69)*. The post shoes are attached with bolts and expanding anchors. At the tops of the posts, metal post caps secure the beams. Rafters are attached to beams with metal rafter anchors. The beam ends overhang the posts below them, and the rafters overhang the beams. Diagonal 100 by 50 mm cross-bracing is fastened with screws to posts and beams; the cross-bracing can be mounted to the inside of the structure if you intend to install sheathing or cladding.

RAFTER ANCHOR

RAFTER

POST CAP

BEAM

CROSS-BRACING

SLAB

POST

POST SHOE

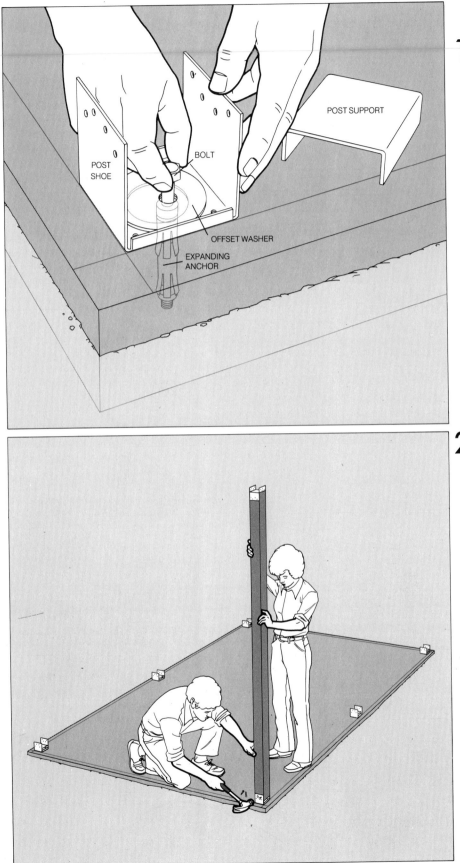

Assembling the Structure

1 **Setting the post shoes.** These U-shaped shoes are bolted to the concrete slab or pier with an offset washer that permits post positions to be shifted for alignment. Place shoes and washers at each post position so that you can outline the washer holes, then drill an 18 mm hole 100 mm deep at each mark and drop an 18 mm expanding anchor into the hole. Replace the post shoe and washer over the hole and, with your fingers, screw a 12 mm bolt 75 mm long into the anchor. Set a post support inside each shoe.

POST SUPPORT

POST SHOE

BOLT

OFFSET WASHER

EXPANDING ANCHOR

2 **Raising the posts.** Nail a post cap to the top of each post and, while a helper holds the post upright on its post support, nail the flanges of the post shoe to the bottom of the post. Use 65 mm galvanized nails.

3 **Plumbing and bracing the corners.** Attach 100 by 50 mm bracing to hold the corner posts plumb while a helper checks with a level. The top of the bracing must be at least 500 mm below the post tops. When corner posts are plumb, tighten the bolts under them *(inset)*.

Mark the tops of the beams for rafters, spacing them as desired but making the first mark so as to position the outside edge of an end rafter flush with the outside edge of a corner post.

4 **Attaching the beams.** Set each beam on top of a row of posts, marked side up, aligning the outermost marks with the outside edges of the corner posts, and get a helper to hold the beam steady while you nail the corner post-cap flanges to the beam. Plumb the inner posts with a level *(right)*, nail them to the post-cap flanges, then tighten the bolts under the posts.

5 **Putting up rafters for an open roof.** Nail a rafter anchor on the top of one beam, to the right of an end-rafter mark. Nail another anchor on the top of the other beam, to the left of the mark. Cut a rafter 500 to 1000 mm longer than the overall width of the structure and set it against the anchors to overhang equally at each side. Nail the rafter to the anchors with 35 mm nails *(right)*. Similarly attach the remaining rafters.

Mark positions for the cross-braces on the posts and beams. On the outside of each post except the corner ones, set the mark at least 300 mm from the top of the post. Mark the top of the beam at least 450 mm to the left and right of the centre line of the post. On each corner post, set the mark at least 450 mm down from the top of the beam, and mark the top of the beam at least 450 mm from the outside edge of the post. Cut 100 by 50 mm braces to fit the marks, angling the ends at a 45-degree angle.

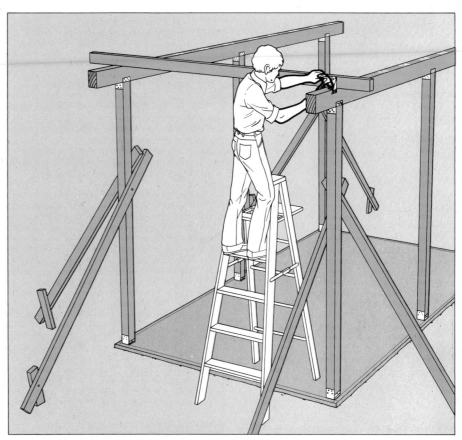

6 **Mounting the braces.** Tack the braces in position, and then secure them with 75 mm No. 10 galvanized screws.

To make post-to-rafter braces at the ends of the structure, mark the corner posts at least 300 mm down from their tops and mark the tops of the end rafters at least 550 mm in from the outer edge of each beam. Cut braces to fit, tack them in place and attach them to the posts with 75 mm No. 10 galvanized screws, and to the rafters with 63 mm No. 10 galvanized screws. Remove the tacking and temporary bracing.

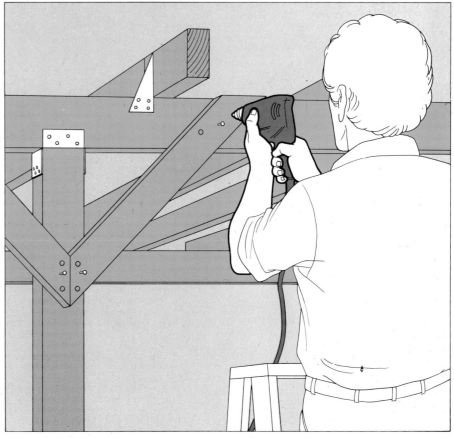

Installing Sloping Roofs

To provide a weathertight roof for an open beam structure, install sloping rather than horizontal rafters and cover them with sheathing and roofing material *(pages 90–91)*. No special calculations are needed; simply estimate the length of the rafters after determining the desired pitch of the roof. This informal kind of carpentry is less precise than the techniques that building a dwelling demand but will serve admirably for a simple outdoor structure.

For a shed roof, build a post-and-beam structure with the posts higher on one side than on the other, bearing in mind that cutting a notch for the lower end of the rafters, as described here, will slightly affect the pitch of your roof. Do not make the fall less than 1 in 75—a pitch of about two degrees—or the slope will not ensure adequate rainfall runoff.

A gable roof is a simple alternative and an appropriate covering for a post-and-beam structure like the one on page 74, which has sides of even height.

Marking rafters for a shed roof. Ask a helper to align a rafter board, on which a chalk line has been snapped down the middle, so that the top of the board touches the top of the higher crossbeam and the chalk line touches the top outer edge of the lower crossbeam. Tack the rafter temporarily to the upper crossbeam, and mark along the outside and top edges of the lower crossbeam for a bird's-mouth cut, a notch that fits the rafter snugly to the crossbeam. Then mark the rafter along the inner face of the upper crossbeam for the ridge cut, the cut that fits the rafter to the upper crossbeam. Using a spirit level, mark a verti-

cal overhang on the end of the rafter that projects beyond the lower crossbeam.

Cut along these three marks then, using this rafter as a template, mark and cut the remaining rafters. Toenail them on 400 mm centres to pre-marked spots on the upper crossbeam, and secure the bird's-mouth cut to the lower beam *(inset)* with metal rafter anchors.

Brace the structure with 150 by 50 mm collar beams secured to each pair of end posts with 75 mm No. 10 screws; toenail another collar beam between the centre posts and reinforce it with angle brackets.

RAFTER BOARD CHALK LINE BIRD'S-MOUTH CUT

Framing a Peaked Roof

1 Marking rafters for a gable roof. Ask a helper to align the rafter board to a crossbeam and a marking guide and, after tacking it to the marking guide, mark the bird's-mouth cut. To construct and place the marking guide, attach a scrap piece of wood the same thickness as the ridge beam and long enough to extend beyond the apex of the roof you envisage to a plank long enough to span the structure. Attach a diagonal brace to both the plank and the marking guide and then position the plank on the crossbeams so that the marking guide is equidistant from them. Finally, tack the plank to both crossbeams. Mark the ridge cut and, using a spirit level, the overhang cut, and then use this board as a template to cut the remaining rafters. Remove the plank and temporary marking guide.

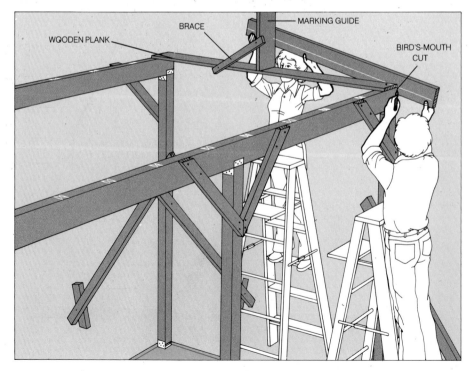

WOODEN PLANK BRACE MARKING GUIDE BIRD'S-MOUTH CUT

2 Assembling the frame. On the ground, cut a 225 by 25 mm ridge board to the same length as the crossbeams and mark it for rafters at 400 mm intervals. Face-nail pre-cut end rafters to one side of it, using three 75 mm galvanized nails for each. Toenail the other end rafters to the opposite side of the board. Brace the structure temporarily with 100 by 50 mm timber face-nailed across the opposite rafters.

3 Setting the frame in place. With three helpers—two at the far end of the roof and one at your end—lift the frame into place, setting the bird's-mouth cuts of the rafters on to the crossbeams. If necessary, remove the temporary bracing to adjust the fit of the rafters, and replace it when they are correctly positioned, then nail the rafters to the rafter anchors *(opposite page, inset)*.

4 Fitting the collar beams. Set a 150 by 50 mm board cut to the width of the structure on top of the crossbeams and against a pair of end rafters, and mark it along the top of the rafters. Cut the board at the marks and use it as a template for the other collar beams. Nail collar beams to the end rafters with six 75 mm galvanized nails.

Mount the rest of the rafters, nailing a pre-cut collar beam to each pair of rafters as you go; then remove the temporary bracing.

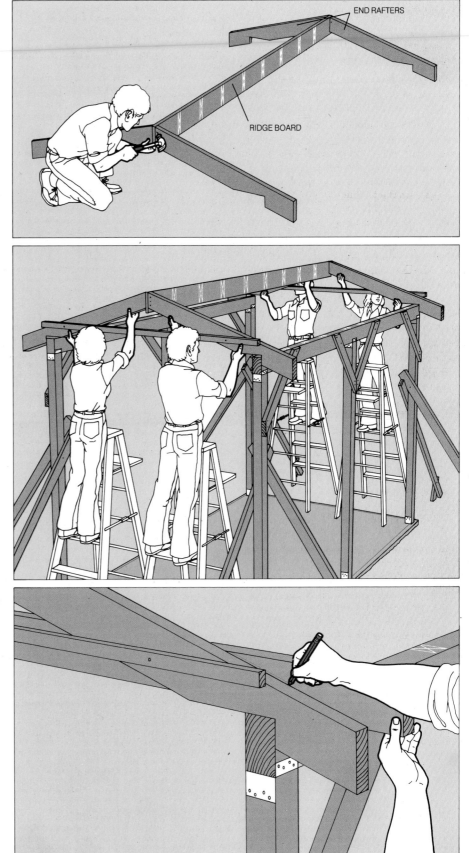

END RAFTERS

RIDGE BOARD

Gazebos: a Bit of Nostalgia

The gazebo—the word is redolent of antique charm—is an open post-and-beam structure, usually of five, six or eight sides, topped with a peaked roof. The Victorians, whose name for this airy summer house is mock-Latin for "I shall gaze", decorated their gazebos with everything from ornately carved scrollwork and wrought-iron ornaments to rustic twigs and branches with the bark left on.

The gazebo is still a popular garden shelter, combining 19th-century charm with the openness and simplicity of conventional post-and-beam structures. Once erected, the structure can be left open or covered with decorative roofing and siding (*pages 90–97*), and it can be ornamented with whatever curlicues the owner fancies.

A gazebo like the one on the right, consisting of a six-sided wooden platform set on concrete blocks, avoids the necessity of casting a slab or setting posts in a perfect hexagon. If the site is uneven, embed the blocks in the earth to level their tops. The six supporting posts are attached to the platform, which is strong enough to bear their weight and that of the beam-and-rafter unit that forms the roof. Install handrails in all but the entrance section, to brace the structure, and set a concrete block in front of the open section as a step.

To determine the length of the platform's sides, measure the radius of however large a circle the platform will occupy. The sides of a hexagon whose points touch the circumference of that circle will be the same as the radius. The gazebo shown here has a roof with a pitch of 37 degrees. To find the distance from the base of the roof to the apex, multiply the radius of the base by 1.25. For a roof of a different pitch, you will need to determine lengths and angles with a detailed scale drawing.

Cut the perimeter boards and crossbeams to the proper length and mitre their ends to an angle of 60 degrees. Cut the spacers (the boards that separate the rafters) to the same angle (*Step 4*). Use a pitchboard (*page 70*) to mark angle cuts at the ends of the rafters. To assemble the roof, you will need to build a nailing platform. Finally, you may want to hire scaffolding to use in lifting the roof into place.

Anatomy of a hexagonal gazebo. Six 75 by 75 mm posts toenailed to a wooden base form the uprights of this post-and-beam structure. The gazebo base, which simply rests on concrete blocks, consists of perimeter boards, floor joists and floorboards, all of 150 by 38 mm timber. Six horizontal crossbeams, five handrails and six plywood arches give the structure lateral rigidity. The 125 by 50 mm roof rafters of the gazebo are nailed at their bases to the crossbeams and attached at their peaks to 100 by 50 mm spacers.

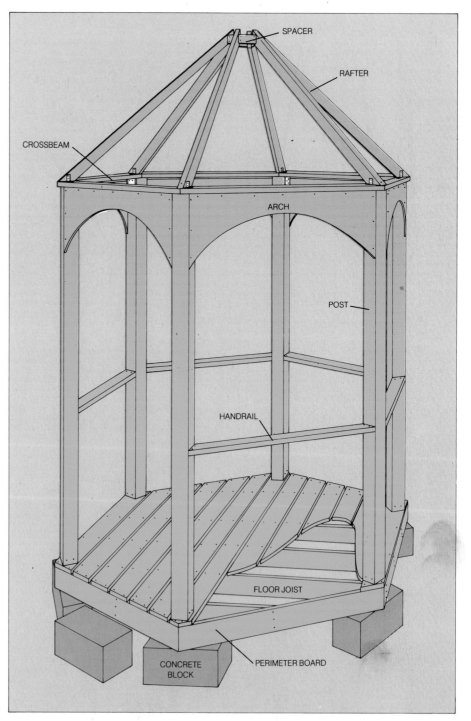

SPACER

RAFTER

CROSSBEAM

ARCH

POST

HANDRAIL

FLOOR JOIST

CONCRETE BLOCK

PERIMETER BOARD

1 Making the base. After cutting both ends of six 150 by 38 mm timbers with a circular saw set to cut an angle of 60 degrees, apply a liberal amount of exterior-grade carpenter's glue to the board ends and assemble the base. Hammer two corrugated frame fasteners into the joints and reinforce the inside joints of the assembled base with 75 mm metal truss plates that have been bent to fit the inside angle of the joints *(inset)*. Assemble the horizontal crossbeams for the roof of the gazebo by the same techniques, and cut the five lengths of 75 by 38 mm handrail.

2 Putting in floor joists. Nail 150 by 38 mm joists, aligned on 400 mm centres, to the gazebo base *(below)*. Cut the joist ends at an angle, where necessary, to match the angle of the perimeter boards. Lay floorboards at right angles to the joists, and trim them with a circular saw *(page 99, Step 3)*. Place six concrete blocks on the ground or on a bed of gravel, to serve as supports for the gazebo base. Use a water level *(page 8)* to even the height of the blocks. Then position the completed base on blocks.

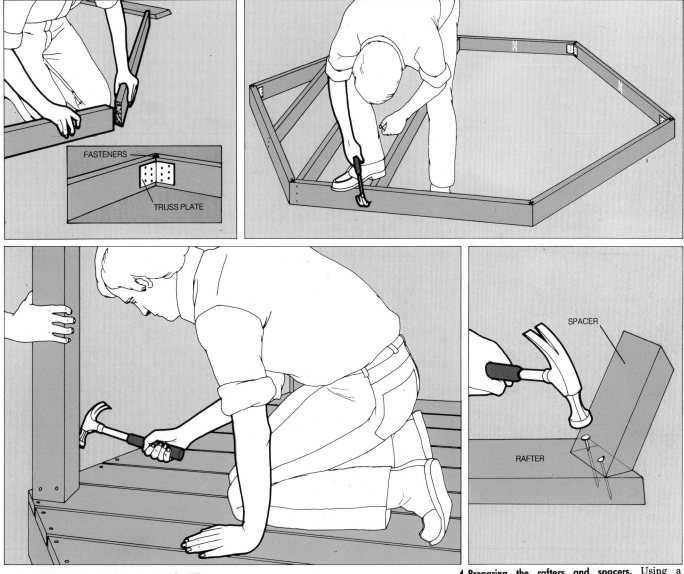

FASTENERS

TRUSS PLATE

SPACER

RAFTER

3 Putting up the posts. After cutting 75 by 75 mm posts to the desired height, toenail the first post to the base with four 75 mm lost-head nails. Plumb and brace the post *(page 36)* and erect and secure the remaining ones, bracing each post to the adjacent one with temporary stiffeners *(overleaf)*.

4 Preparing the rafters and spacers. Using a protractor or a pitchboard *(page 70)*, mark the ends of six 125 by 50 mm rafters to match a roof with a pitch of 37 degrees. Cut them to the distance from the base of the roof to the apex, less 250 mm. Then cut the ends of six 100 by 50 mm spacer boards to the same angle as the perimeter boards, measuring them so that the length of their short sides equals 160 mm. Toenail one spacer to the peak end of each rafter while it rests on the ground *(above)*.

5 **Assembling the roof frame.** Position the base of the first rafter board over a joint of the crossbeam roof base, toenail the rafter in place with a 75 mm round-wire nail and secure the connection with 50 mm angle brackets. Attach a second rafter with its spacer as you did the first, then toenail the free end of the first spacer to the open end of the second rafter. To facilitate nailing, slip a temporary platform—built with 100 by 50 mm timber to the exact height of the spacers above the crossbeams—underneath the spacers, and brace the edge of the rafter with your leg. Add the remaining rafters and spacers the same way.

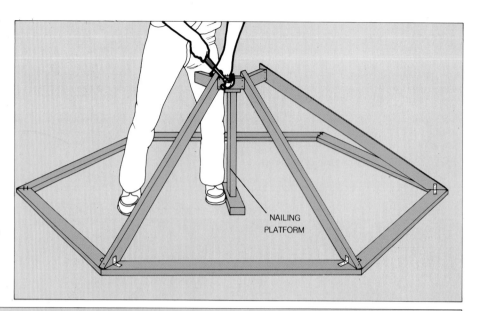

NAILING PLATFORM

6 **Placing the roof.** Get two helpers to hand the roof up to you and a third helper standing at the ends of two sets of scaffolding, placed at opposite sides of the gazebo. Carefully walk the roof into place; position it with the outer edges of the crossbeams resting on the corners of the posts.

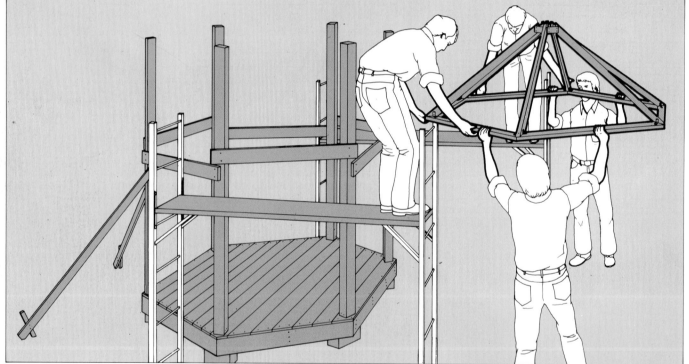

7 **Fastening the roof.** Drive a 75 mm round-wire nail through the ends of all the crossbeams and into the top of each post *(right)*. Then nail a 75 mm metal angle plate to both sides of each post with 25 mm round-wire nails *(far right)*.

Attach the handrails to the posts with angle brackets. Fasten 25 by 25 mm nailing blocks to the underside of the crossbeams and install plywood or chipboard arches, cut at a 60-degree angle to fit between posts.

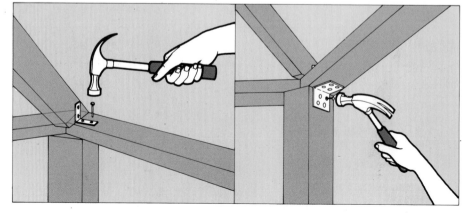

Tree Houses: Perches for Young Adventurers

Children love tree houses of all shapes and sizes, whether they are mere platforms or elaborate arboreal hideaways complete with doors, windows and pulleys to raise and lower picnic baskets.

Tree-house platforms may be attached to strong limbs of a low-branching tree on top of horizontal crossbeams. The design has to suit the tree—a tree with three main branches going off at angles is easiest to work with. Alternatively, the tree-house platform can be set on freestanding posts.

Safety comes first in designing and building tree houses. Even the most care-fully built ones are subject to unusual stresses, and their height is a hazard. A tree house made for small children should be no more than 2.5 to 3 metres off the ground, and should be located within sight of the main dwelling. Guard rails at least 900 mm high round the sides of any elevated structure are a mandatory safety feature. Securely fix a rope or rung ladder to the entrance hatch or, where possible, nail a series of 50 by 50 mm cleats to the tree trunk. As an additional measure to cushion the shock of an accidental fall, rake the ground beneath the structure free of rocks, then line it with a 50 to 75 mm layer of sand or the pulverized bark used to keep weeds down in flower beds.

When attaching a platform frame to a tree, inspect all the branches that you will nail into, to make sure that the tree wood is free from rot, and later check periodically to make sure that high winds or tree growth have not weakened a supporting brace of the platform. Apply tree-wound paint wherever you cut away branches. Do not skimp on nailing; the nails will not hurt the tree if you spread tree-wound paint round them.

A structure nailed to branches. A typical tree-house platform, attached to a tree that has strong, spreading limbs, rests on 150 by 50 mm crossbeams nailed between the branches and is braced with 100 by 50 mm boards attached to the tree and to the platform frame. The base of the tree house is a framed deck of 150 by 25 mm boards secured to 150 by 50 mm joists set at 400 mm centres. When building the base, leave one of the end boards out so that the platform can be hoisted into the tree *(page 84, Step 2)*. Guard rails and garden fencing add security.

A small roofed structure, here sheathed with plywood, occupies part of the deck; a ladder gives access to an entrance hatch cut in the platform.

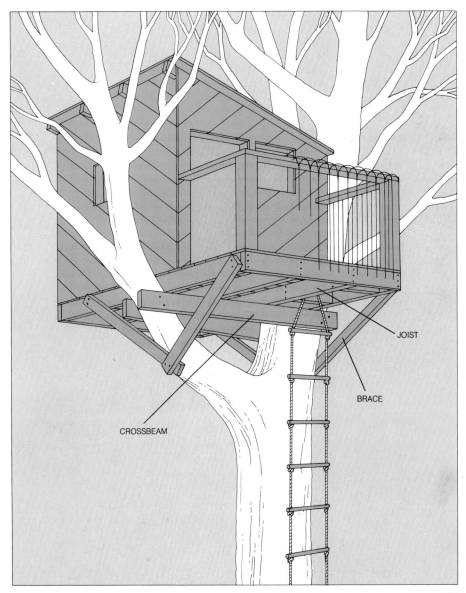

JOIST

BRACE

CROSSBEAM

Hoisting and Securing the Platform

1 **Installing crossbeams.** Select a site for the platform. With the aid of a helper, nail two or three 150 by 50 mm horizontal crossbeams to the tree at the same height and level. Work from ladders steadied against scraps of timber. Measure carefully the space that the platform will occupy on the crossbeams.

2 **Raising the platform.** Loop a length of nylon rope round one frame member and use a pulley to hoist the platform up to the crossbeams. With assistance from two helpers on ladders, set the platform in position on the crossbeams. Secure it by toenailing down from the platform sides into the crossbeams, and up from the crossbeams into the joists.

3 **Bracing the platform.** Nail at least three diagonal 100 by 50 mm braces between the sides of the platform and the tree. Each brace must meet the platform at an angle of not less than 45 degrees. In order to provide reasonably good nailing surfaces for the braces, you may have to trim their ends somewhat until you achieve an appropriate fit. Or you may have to nail a cleat to the tree or the platform and then attach the end of the brace to the cleat.

A Deck Built Round a Tree

A freestanding platform. For trees that have high-branching trunks, build an elevated deck, supported by 100 by 100 mm posts anchored in concrete *(page 37)*. To make the platform frame, secure 150 by 50 mm boards with coach screws in 15 mm deep notches in the outer faces of the posts. Secure 150 by 50 mm joists between opposite sides of the frame with nails or joist hangers. Nail trimmers round the gap in the frame where the tree trunk will be, and round the entrance hatch. Attach diagonal braces from the posts to the frame with coach screws. Then nail 150 by 25 mm flooring boards directly to the joists, leaving a small gap round the tree trunk. Make a guard rail of 100 by 50 mm timber and enclose the open space between the rail and the deck with wooden or metal fencing.

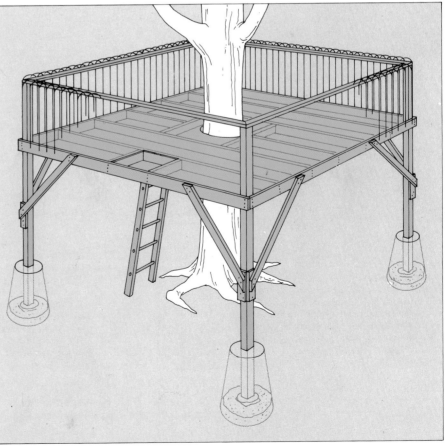

The Dome: a Sturdy Bubble of Wooden Triangles

The geodesic dome, which was invented by Buckminster Fuller in 1951, ingeniously combines equal-sided isosceles triangles into a pattern of hexagons and pentagons to form a hemisphere that is larger and stronger than any conventional structure that can be built with the same quantity of identical materials.

A dome like the one shown on the following pages, which is easily built of 25 by 25 mm wooden struts stapled together, is cheap, strong, attractive and versatile. It can span up to 9 metres without internal bracing, making it ideal for almost any garden shelter calling for light, airy, uninterrupted interior space. It makes a fine cover for a swimming pool, to keep out airborne debris and to warm the water by trapping solar heat. A door or window can be created simply by hinging one of the

dome's triangles *(page 89, Step 7)*; to keep the structure strong, however, never hinge two adjacent triangles.

This particular dome is a fair-weather structure, difficult to leak-proof but easy to disassemble for off-season storage. Building it involves three simple, repetitive operations: cutting the struts, assembling them into triangles and attaching the triangles to one another. Cutting the struts to the right length is a matter of applying the table on the right; mitring strut ends to the correct angles is easy to do with a home-made jig *(opposite page, Step 1)*.

The angles given for the strut ends will result in triangles with slight gaps at the corners opening to the inside of the triangle frame. This ensures that the tips of the struts will meet and the outside dimensions of the triangles will be exact.

Before assembling the dome, prepare its cover by wrapping each triangle with a flexible covering or attaching a triangular piece of plywood or rigid plastic. Use flexible, ultraviolet-resistant plastic on light-trapping domes for pools and greenhouses, coloured plastic for providing shade. A fine wire or plastic mesh keeps insects out; a medium mesh keeps birds out—or in.

Plastic-sheathed domes can be partly weatherproofed by sealing all joints with plastic tape, but will still leak round windows and doors. As plastic or other covering deteriorates, replace it by removing and re-covering affected frames.

In windy locations, cut 75 mm hardboard reinforcement discs with a compass or keyhole saw and screw them to the struts where the points of triangles meet, using one 25 mm wood screw per strut.

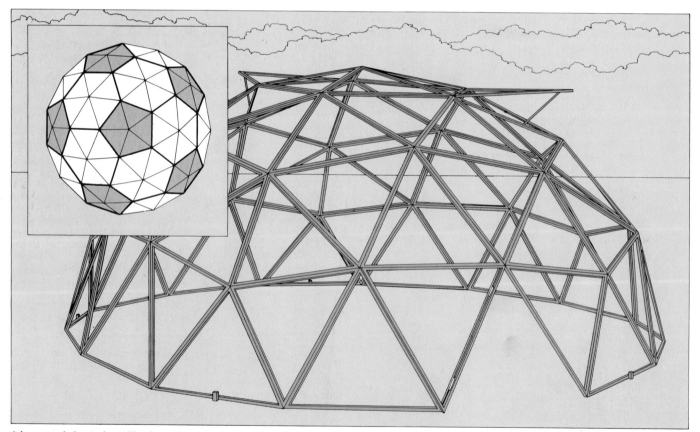

A home-made hemisphere. The dome shown here is composed of two sizes of triangular wooden frames made from straight, knot-free planed-all-round 25 by 25 mm timber. It is covered with clear plastic and has hinged vents and a door opening. Seen from above *(inset)*, the dome is a pattern of pentagons formed from short triangles (grey) and hexagons formed from tall triangles (white). Each kind of triangle has two legs of equal length and a base of a different length. The bases are the heavy lines of the inset; the legs converge at the centres of the hexagons and pentagons. The lengths of the legs and bases vary with the size of the dome but the angles at which they meet *(opposite, Step 1)* are always the same.

Finding the Lengths of Struts for a Dome

Diameter of dome	Height	Tall triangle struts		Short triangle struts	
		Base	Leg	Base	Leg
3m	1.2m	605mm	619mm	605mm	523mm
4.5m	1.8m	908mm	928mm	908mm	784mm
6m	2.4m	1211mm	1237mm	1211mm	1046mm
7.5m	3m	1513mm	1546mm	1513mm	1307mm
9m	3.6m	1816mm	1856mm	1816mm	1569mm

Domes cut to order. Make a dome in any of five sizes by cutting the struts to the lengths indicated in the table on the left. Read down the left side of the table to find the diameter and height of the dome you want to make; read across to find the length of each strut from tip to tip of the mitred ends. Make 30 bases for short triangles and 60 legs; make 45 bases for tall triangles and 90 legs.

Cutting and Assembling the Framework

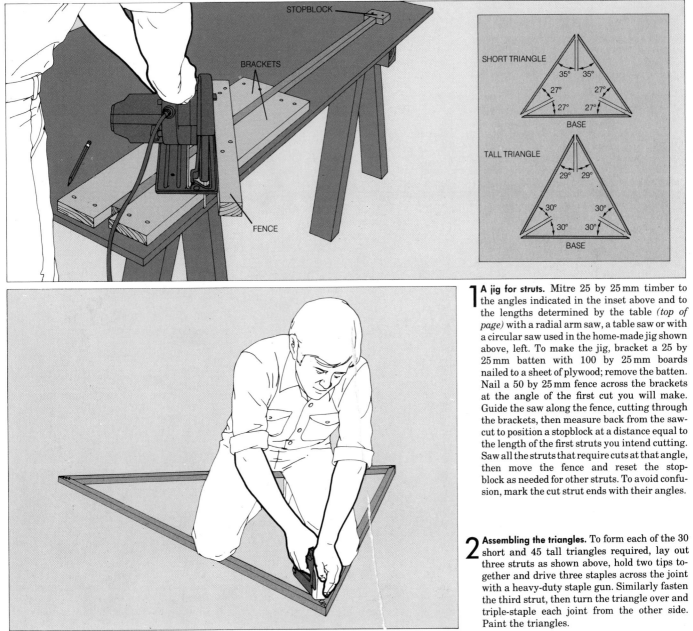

STOPBLOCK

BRACKETS

FENCE

SHORT TRIANGLE
35° 35°
27° 27°
27° 27°
BASE

TALL TRIANGLE
29° 29°
30° 30°
30° 30°
BASE

1 **A jig for struts.** Mitre 25 by 25 mm timber to the angles indicated in the inset above and to the lengths determined by the table *(top of page)* with a radial arm saw, a table saw or with a circular saw used in the home-made jig shown above, left. To make the jig, bracket a 25 by 25 mm batten with 100 by 25 mm boards nailed to a sheet of plywood; remove the batten. Nail a 50 by 25 mm fence across the brackets at the angle of the first cut you will make. Guide the saw along the fence, cutting through the brackets, then measure back from the saw-cut to position a stopblock at a distance equal to the length of the first struts you intend cutting. Saw all the struts that require cuts at that angle, then move the fence and reset the stop-block as needed for other struts. To avoid confusion, mark the cut strut ends with their angles.

2 **Assembling the triangles.** To form each of the 30 short and 45 tall triangles required, lay out three struts as shown above, hold two tips together and drive three staples across the joint with a heavy-duty staple gun. Similarly fasten the third strut, then turn the triangle over and triple-staple each joint from the other side. Paint the triangles.

3 **Covering the triangles.** Lay a triangle on a sheet of plastic, fold the plastic up over one strut and staple it near a corner. Stretch the plastic slightly along the strut to a second corner and staple it. Repeat for the other two struts; avoid leaving wrinkles at the corners. Then gently stretch the plastic and staple it to the rest of each strut, starting at the middle and working towards the ends. Trim off excess plastic.

To cover a triangle with rigid plastic or other solid material, lay the triangle on the material and trace round the edge. Cut the material along the traced lines and fasten it to the triangle with weatherproof staples, nails or screws.

4 **Assembling the first course.** At a level site, hold two tall triangles edge to edge with their bases orientated as shown. Align the corners and staple the two inside edges together every 100 to 150 mm. Attach a third tall triangle to the right side of the second, orientated as shown in the inset. Continuing to the right, similarly attach three short triangles with the bases orientated as indicated in the inset. While helpers hold the triangles upright, add four more sets of tall and short triangles to the first set to form a circular fence leaning inwards, with its plastic-covered side outwards; staple the last triangle to the first.

Measure along the ground from the middle of the base of a short triangle to the point opposite it where the corners of three tall triangles meet near ground level. Make similar measurements in different directions and adjust the assembly of triangles to make all the measurements equal.

5 **Staking down the dome.** Drive a 600 mm long 50 by 50 mm wooden stake treated with a preservative into the ground alongside the middle of the base strut of a short triangle—one of the five points at which the dome's base sits firmly on the ground. Secure the stake to the strut with a galvanized wood screw. Similarly stake down the base struts of the other four short triangles.

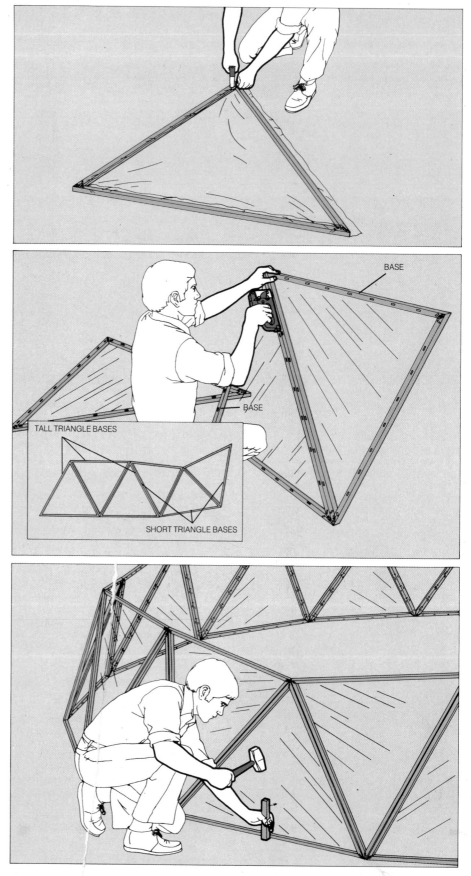

BASE

BASE

TALL TRIANGLE BASES

SHORT TRIANGLE BASES

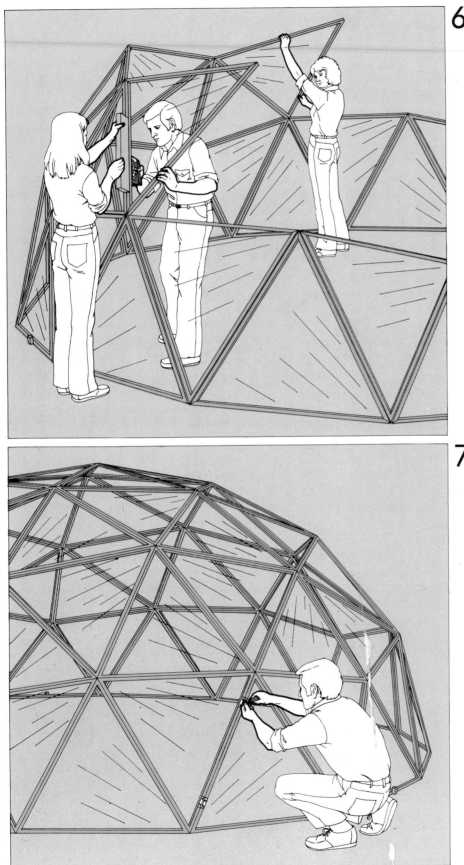

6 Finishing the dome. Following the pattern in the inset on page 86, install additional courses of triangles. Use a helper to hand in triangles, to help position them and to hold a block of wood opposite the staple gun to ensure that the staples penetrate well. Get two others to help keep the sides of the dome upright until you have completed the second course. When the sides of the dome rise too high to pass triangles over, make an opening in the dome by removing a tall base-down triangle from the first course. Installing the last few triangles may require you and your helper to stand on stepladders. If the last pair of triangles do not fit, release the dome from the stake to fit the triangles in.

7 Making a door. Reattach with hinges the tall triangle you removed during construction. Reinforce with vinyl tape the opening edges of the door and the edges of the adjacent triangles that form the unhinged side of the doorjamb. Screw strips of wood to the jamb to form a doorstop. Latch the door with hooks and eyes.

Similarly make hinged windows. Alternatively, door and window openings can be made simply by removing individual frames.

A Wide Choice of Coverings for Top and Sides

How you choose to enclose an outdoor structure depends upon both the type of building and the purpose for which it was made. Lightweight coverings—which are often more attractive and functional than the fully weatherproof roofs and sides that are used for more substantial buildings—frequently suffice for auxiliary buildings. To a great extent, the coverings depend on the construction method used: for an A-frame, the roof is also the side walls; for a simple dome, very light covering provides the roof and the walls.

While a rainproof roof is necessary for a storage shed, many other structures—lawn pavilions, summer houses and the like—are more pleasant with open roofs. Open rafters, with decorative end cuts, may be enough alone or they can be joined by crosspieces in an attractive pattern. For more shade, you can cover the rafters with latticework or rows of slats, or use some more exotic material such as blind cloth or woven reed *(pages 96–97)*. These materials can also be used for the sides.

A rainproof roof can be made of corrugated plastic panels or, alternatively, from chipboard covered with layers of roofing felt. If you decide to use roofing felt *(opposite page)*, choose a variety with a polyester rather than a rag or glass base; it will last much longer. For a decorative finish, use a felt with a mineralized surface, available in green, blue-grey or red. Always unroll the felt at least half an hour before use, and never install it in cold or wet weather.

Plastic panels *(page 92)* are made of either PVC or fibreglass-reinforced plastic. PVC roofing comes in transparent, translucent and opaque panels, while fibreglass is available only in a translucent form. PVC is the cheaper option but—unless it is reinforced with wire—it will break more easily than fibreglass. Both types of panel come in standard widths, generally 750 mm. Most builders' merchants stock these sheets in 1800 mm to 3 metre lengths, and longer lengths can be ordered specially if required. They can be cut to size with a fine-toothed handsaw. Install the sheets in courses, starting at the low edge of the roof, and overlap courses in order to make the roof watertight. Manufacturers supply scalloped filler strips that match the profile of their panels; fixings vary but are usually specially designed waterproof screw-and-washer devices, driven into the ridges of the panels.

Many types of covering can be used to weatherproof sides, including the popular shiplap and feather-edged boards. The board-and-batten method of covering exterior walls *(page 95)* uses readily available square-edged timber, which sheds rainwater well and allows timber to shrink and expand without affecting its weather resistance. As a general rule, however, make sure that any timber used for exterior work is pressure-treated.

A floor often can be dispensed with, particularly for summer structures such as pergolas or pavilions. You can use the ground as it is, cover it with gravel, sand or paving stones, or pour a lightweight concrete slab. A slab is necessary for storage purposes but, for leisure use, a wooden floor is generally more comfortable. Unless the structure is going to be fairly weathertight, such wooden floors are generally made slatted, in order to provide spaces for drainage *(pages 98–99)*.

Custom Cuts for Rafters

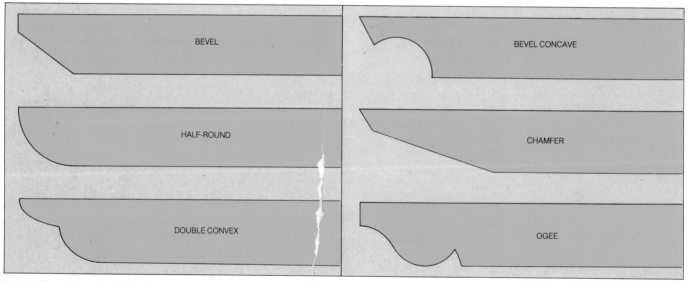

Designs for rafter ends. These six patterns are the most popular for adding a decorative touch to the plain ends of open-structure rafters. They also serve to shed rainwater from the end-grain of the rafters. Enlarge the pattern you plan to use on graph paper and transfer it to a rafter. Use a jigsaw with a rough-cut blade for the cuts.

Simple Roofing That is Weatherproof

1 **Laying roofing felt.** Nail chipboard sheathing to the rafters, making certain that nail heads are well sunk in and that all rough edges are planed down. Using galvanized clout nails at 450 mm intervals, secure the upper edge of a full-width strip of roofing felt so that it overlaps the eave by 50 mm. Fold it back so you can spread 300 mm wide borders of adhesive on the sheathing. Press the strip firmly in place, leaving the overlap hanging down to serve as a drip, and secure it to the edge of the sheathing with nails.

Apply additional strips of felt in the same way, allowing a 10 mm overlap of each upper strip over the strip below, until the roof is covered.

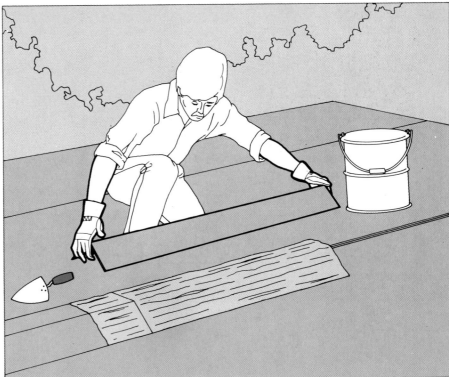

2 **Laying ridge pieces.** On a gable roof, cut pieces of roofing felt 1000 by 300 mm and use adhesive to secure them along the ridge, overlapping each piece by 150 mm *(right)*. Nail the last 150 mm of each piece to the roof, so that adhesive and the succeeding piece cover the nail heads.

On a single-pitch roof, let the top strip overlap the upper edge of the chipboard sheath by 125 mm. Fold the overlap around the sheath edge and nail or staple it to the face of the upper crossbeam.

A Translucent, Rainproof Roof

1 **Attaching the filler strips.** Install a fascia board and nail cross supports between the rafters at 1 metre intervals. Nail or glue the scalloped filler strips along the top of the fascia board *(right)* and on top of the cross supports.

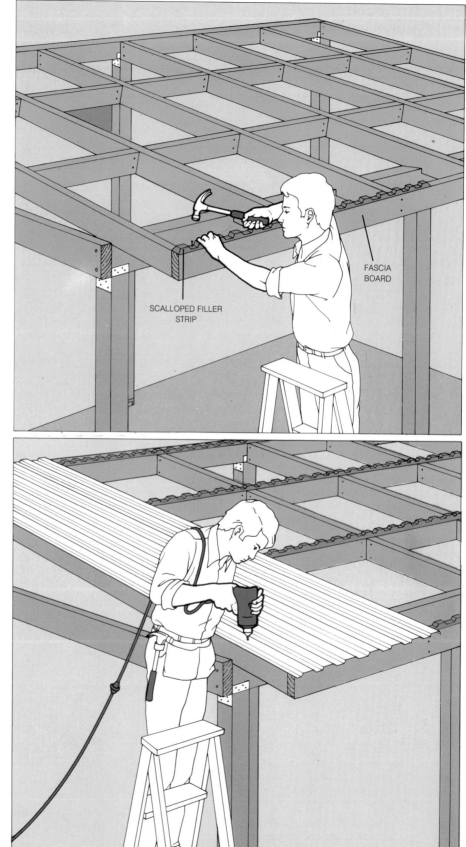

FASCIA
BOARD

SCALLOPED FILLER
STRIP

2 **Installing the panels.** Beginning at the lowest point on the slope of the roof, lay the first sheet over the rafters so that the last ridge of the corrugated plastic sheet lies over the end rafter. Caution: in high-wind areas, always lay the first panel farthest from the direction of the prevailing wind. Drill holes slightly smaller than your screws through every second ridge along the fascia and the cross supports—approximately every 200 mm in panels where the ridges are close together—and along the end rafters every 200 to 300 mm *(right)*. Secure the panels with the fixing screws provided by the manufacturer. Overlap successive sheets by two ridges, pre-drilling and screwing them together into the fascia board and cross supports.

If you are sheathing a gable-roofed structure, the ridge-beam edge of the panels should be secured after you have installed aluminium ridge-roll flashing.

Openwork Roofs
for Light Shade

Slats for shades. Nail parallel rows of 50 by 25 mm timber to rafters, using a slat as a spacer and working down if the roof is pitched. To make a safe working platform on the roof, temporarily nail to the rafters a sheet of chipboard with a 50 by 25 mm footstop along the lower edge. Move the platform as you work down the roof; near the eaves, finish the job from a ladder.

Staggered eggcrate crosspieces. For a distinctive open overhead pattern, mark for crosspieces between horizontal rafters, using a tape measure and combination square. Cut the crosspieces from boards of the same dimension as the rafters and face-nail through the rafters into the end-grain of the crosspieces.

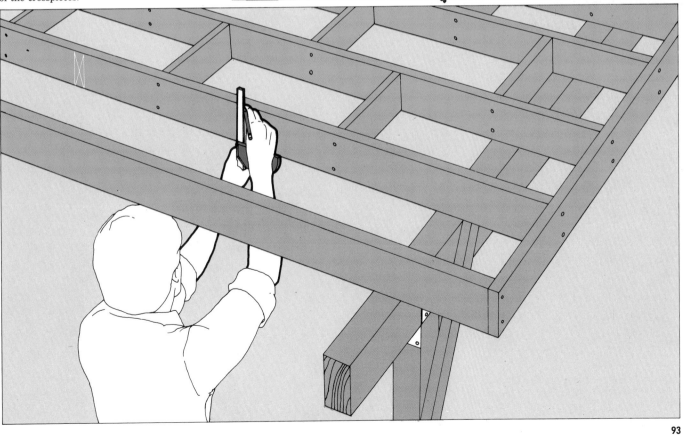

Installing Latticework

1 Laying out the lattice. Cut pieces of lath to approximate lengths for a criss-cross pattern, then staple them at a 45-degree angle to the sides of a rectangular frame of 25 by 25 mm battens, using a length of lath as a spacer. Cut off the protruding ends of the lath evenly with a jigsaw.

2 Attaching the frame. Using panel pins or lost-head nails, secure the lattice frame against 25 by 25 mm or 50 by 25 mm stops nailed along the inside edges of the structure's framework. Use a pin hammer for greater accuracy.

Strong Walls of Boards and Battens

1 Securing the bearers. Toenail 50 by 50 mm horizontal bearers at 400 mm centres, flush with the outer faces of the posts. Leave a gap of at least 50 mm between the bottom bearer and the slab, to prevent damage from damp.

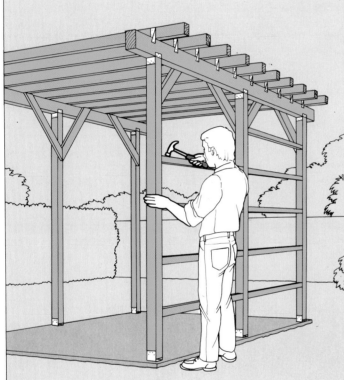

2 Installing the boards. Lay strips of 6 mm plywood between the posts on the slab. Secure 100 by 19 mm boards vertically to the bearers, resting their bottom ends on the strip of plywood and using one galvanized nail per bearer for each board. Start from the middle of each side and set the boards 10 mm apart using a strip of plywood as a spacer *(below)*. When you are four or five boards from a corner, slightly adjust the spacing between boards so that the last board will lie flush with the outside of a post.

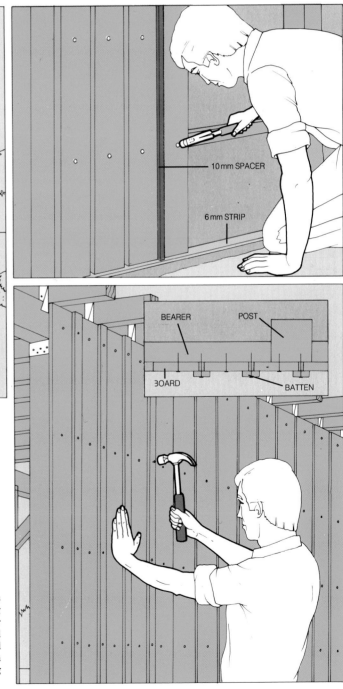

10 mm SPACER

6 mm STRIP

BEARER   POST

BOARD   BATTEN

3 Closing the gaps. Secure 38 by 12 mm battens along the gaps between the boards, nailing through the centre of each batten into the bearer or post behind *(inset)*. When you have completed the sides, remove the 6 mm scrap of plywood and fill the space between the wall and the slab with sealant which will keep out water while allowing for some movement in the timber.

Airy Sheathing, Easy to Mount

For outdoor structures that you plan to use only in warm weather, decorative materials such as blind cloth, woven reed and bamboo provide ideal coverings. Although they will not keep out heavy rain, they provide an attractive and airy environment which is especially suitable for structures like domes, trellises or tree houses. Light in weight and comparatively easy to install, these summer sheathings can be attached with minimal support to almost any type of existing framework.

Water-resistant blind cloth, which is made from synthetic canvas, affords the greatest degree of privacy. Manufactured in a variety of weaves that admit different amounts of light, blind cloth also provides an ideal screen for shade-loving plants. Ready-made blinds in many sizes and styles are available at blind and awning retailers; these may provide you with suitable wall coverings. For the custom-made roof covering shown below, however, blind cloth must be specially ordered from a manufacturer, who will cut it to size, reinforce the sides and install eyelets to your particular specifications. Order blind cloth cut 100 mm smaller all round than your roof so that you can lace it in place. Specify reinforced edges with one eyelet in each corner, two 75 mm from each corner and the rest spaced at 450 mm intervals.

Bamboo and woven reed are both more natural-looking than blind cloth and can be trimmed to size with metal shears. They are sold in rolls of varying lengths and widths, for use as both roof and wall coverings. For a roof, they can be sandwiched between 25 by 25 mm battens and galvanized wire (opposite page, above and centre). For wall coverings, they can be stapled to removable 50 by 50 mm frames. The bamboo and reed blinds sold for use on windows can be applied to side openings.

If you intend to use reed or bamboo frames for a post-and-beam structure, install cross-braces on the inside rather than the outside of the posts (page 77).

Using Blind Cloth, Bamboo and Woven Reed

Attaching blind cloth. To lace blind cloth to a roof, install 90 mm eyebolts in the corners, stretch the pre-cut fabric across the roof and tie each corner eyelet to its corresponding eyebolt using a double reef knot. Screw additional eyebolts along the sides of the roof, lining them up opposite the eyelets in the cloth.

Tie one end of a length of synthetic cord to a corner eyebolt and lace the free end of the cord through the corner eyelet to the next eyebolt, from there to the adjacent eyelet, and so on to the end of the side. Similarly lace the opposite side. With a helper, hand-tighten the lacing on both sides, keeping the fabric centred between the exterior rafters. Similarly lace and hand-tighten the two remaining sides.

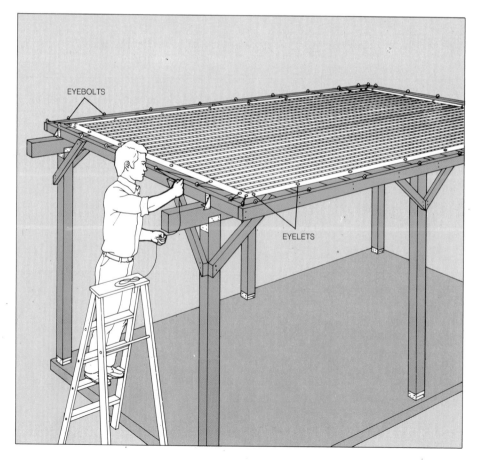

Roofing with bamboo and woven reed. After installing 90 mm eyebolts every 500 to 600 mm along the tops of the end rafters, stretch galvanized 18-gauge wires across the roof and tie them to opposite eyebolts *(left, above)*. Place the bamboo or woven reed on top of the wires and lay 25 by 25 mm battens on top of your roofing material, along the path of the wires.

Fasten the battens every 1000 to 1200 mm with lengths of 22-gauge wire threaded through the roofing and round the 18-gauge wire below, and then secured with a twist at the top of the battens *(left, below)*.

Walls of bamboo or woven reed. Screw 50 by 50 mm bearers flush with the support posts *(far left)*: the corner bearers flush with the outside of the building *(inset)*, the centre bearers flush with the sides of the intermediate posts. Screw 50 mm angle brackets at the top, centre and bottom of each bearer. Cut three more bearers to fit between each set of vertical bearers. Place them horizontally between the angle brackets and screw them in position.

Cut the wall covering flush with the outer edges of the frame. While a helper holds the covering in place, staple the top corner to the frame with 25 mm galvanized staples *(left)*, then staple it every 150 mm along the top, sides and bottom.

Wooden Floors for Comfort

Floors are an integral part of some structures: the gazebo and tree house both depend on their floors for support. Other buildings which rest on underground footings or a concrete slab, as does the post-and-beam structure on pages 74–79, are built without floors and may not need any. But, to provide a dry and ventilated surface to walk on, or to serve as a platform for storage, an additional wooden floor may be desirable. For a permanent floor, build an understructure as shown on the right, above. For a removable floor, build portable modules, called duckboards, to rest on the ground or slab *(opposite, below)*.

The surface can be either 100 by 38 mm or 150 by 38 mm boards, spaced 5 mm apart for good drainage. Laid flat, these boards are normally nailed to 150 by 50 mm joists spaced at 400 mm centres.

Wherever possible, lay the boards so that the rings which are visible in the end grain are in a "U" shape; then, if the board warps, it will bend in the opposite direction to the ring lines and shed water easily. And you can avoid splitting the board ends when nailing by first blunting the nail points with a hammer.

The concrete piers which support the post-and-beam structure on these pages help prevent rot by raising the floor off the ground. Piers are made with a simple wooden form *(page 69)*.

Adding a Permanent Floor

1 Building the understructure for a floor. Attach 150 by 50 mm boards with coach screws to the outsides of the posts, then nail joist hangers inside this frame for 150 by 50 mm interior joists spaced 400 mm apart. After you have installed the joists, nail 150 by 50 mm strutting between them in a staggered pattern. Finally, attach nailing blocks to the posts of the structure at the height of the joists to provide support for the floorboards whose ends will butt the posts.

NAILING BLOCK

STRUTTING

2 Fastening the boards. Nail floorboards to the joists, spacing them 5 mm apart. As you proceed, use a steel tape measure to make sure that the boards are not drifting out of parallel with the understructure. If you find a deviation, correct it by slightly adjusting the angle of the next few boards. Caution: make sure that these angle adjustments come well within the floor area; the final floorboard must align precisely with the end of the understructure.

3 **Squaring the end boards.** It is generally easier to lay the boards of a floor without trying to line up edges exactly—the lengths of pieces vary quite considerably—then square off all the ends together with a circular saw. Using a handsaw, first trim an end board to the overhang you prefer—up to 50 mm is usual—then nail a straight scrap of timber across the boards as a cutting jig so that the left edge of the saw's horizontal platform, or shoe, guides the blade.

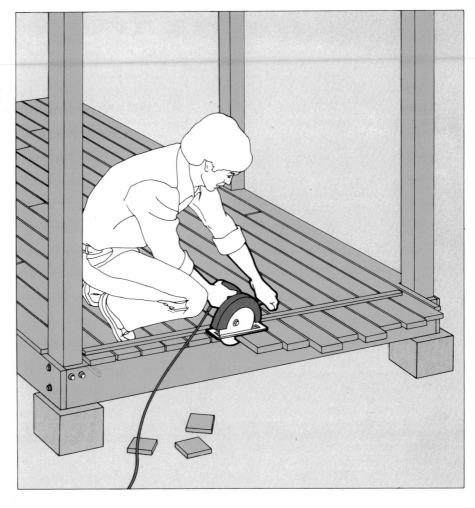

Putting Together a Portable Platform

Making a duckboard floor. Face-nail 100 by 38 mm floorboards to a 1-metre-square understructure, made by butt-nailing pressure-treated 100 by 50 mm boards. Space the floorboards about 5 mm apart, using a strip of plywood as a spacer, but adjust the spacing of the last few boards so that the outermost board fits the end of the frame precisely.

Make as many of these miniature platforms as you need to cover the floor, adjusting size to fit.

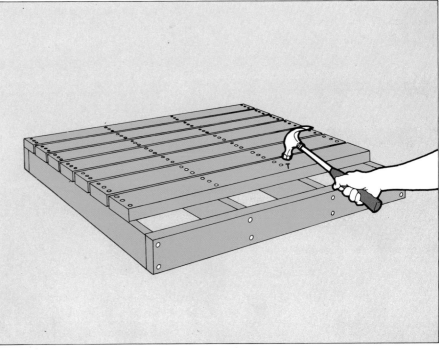

A Glassed-In Framework to Nurture Seedlings

A cold frame looks just like a low box set flat in the ground. It is, in fact, a miniature greenhouse with a hinged glass or plastic roof. Within the cold frame, soil and air are warmed by the sun's rays even while the temperature outside the frame is below freezing, and this means that you can start to grow seedlings long before the beginning of the proper growing season. When spring comes, you can replant the seedlings elsewhere in the garden and enjoy flowers, fruits and vegetables far sooner than unaided nature would allow.

For the cold frame's top, or sash, you can make use of an old window. Construct the walls from rot-resistant cedar, from less expensive wood treated with a wood preservative or from exterior-grade plywood, matching the dimensions of the wall to the size of the sash. For larger cold frames, use two or more windows, mounted side by side. If you do not have a spare window and cannot buy an old one at a reasonable cost, build a frame of 50 by 50 mm timber and cover each face of the frame with a sheet of plastic. Air trapped between the two sheets of plastic provides insulation for the cold frame.

Slope the side walls of the frame from a height of 300 mm at the back to 150 mm at the front, and set the frame facing south, so that the roof slants towards the noon sun. Treat all wooden parts that are not naturally rot-resistant with copper naphthenate, a preservative that does not harm plants; do not use creosote, penta-chlorophenol or mercury compounds to preserve the wood—they are all toxic to plants. Paint the inside of the frame white so it will reflect the sun's light and heat.

Finally, install a prop to hold the sash open for cooling—a temperature higher than 20°C inside the frame could injure the seedlings. The design shown here will hold the sash securely even on windy days. To stop excess heat loss on frosty nights, drape a tarpaulin over the cold frame or pile leaves or straw round it.

You can, if you like, convert your cold frame to a hotbed and warm the plants with a heating cable and thermostat, available from garden centres. Dig out the soil inside the frame to 150 mm, add a 50 mm layer of sand and zigzag the heating cable on the sand. To protect the cable, cover it with 10 mm plastic mesh, then cover the mesh with 100 to 150 mm of soil.

1 Making the side walls. Lay a window sash on a length of 300 by 50 mm plywood or timber with one corner touching a line marking the height of the frame front above the lower edge of the board and the other protruding 5 mm beyond an upper corner. Mark the diagonal and cut along it to make one frame side, then use the cut board as a template to cut the other side. For the back and front of the frame, cut a 300 by 50 mm and a 150 by 50 mm board to match the length of the winddow sash less the thickness of the frame sides.

HEIGHT AT FRONT OF FRAME

2 Assembling the frame. Screw the side boards to the front and back pieces, plane the top edges of the front and back to match the side slope, and anchor the frame in the ground. Dig a 50 mm trench in the soil, sink the frame in place, then drive 50 by 50 mm stakes at the inside corners, using 450 mm stakes at the back and 300 mm stakes at the front. Attach the frame to the stakes with wood screws. Use butt hinges to attach the window to the back of the frame.

3 Rigging the prop sticks. Glue four 10 mm dowels into holes bored towards the front of the frame and sash sides *(below)*, using dowels 125 mm long in the frame and 100 mm long in the sash. Drill 3 mm holes through the dowels. Make two prop sticks from 600 mm lengths of 50 by 25 mm timber, drilled with 15 mm holes every 50 mm. Slip the sticks over the dowels to hold the window open and push split pins through the dowel holes to secure the sticks *(bottom)*.

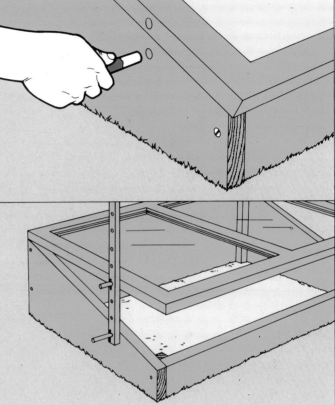

Tips for Using a Greenhouse Kit

The easiest way to add a full-scale greenhouse to your garden is to buy one in kit form. Timber or aluminium-framed models, either lean-to or freestanding, are available in a variety of sizes to suit any property or price range.

Aluminium-framed greenhouses are strong, long-lasting and good value for money. Many people, however, prefer the traditional appearance of a timber frame. Rot-resistant cedar is attractive and durable but costly. Softwood-framed greenhouses cost approximately the same as aluminium-framed ones, but they will deteriorate unless they are treated regularly with a timber preservative (choose one that is harmless to plants).

Any greenhouse requires a firm, level foundation. With all but the smallest models—which can be anchored directly to the ground—it is wise to prepare a plinth of blocks, treated timber or concrete, at least 200 mm wide and set about 150 mm into the earth. Attach the base of the greenhouse frame to the plinth, using the manufacturer's fixings. For a foundation that includes a solid floor, lay a concrete slab *(page 69)*.

Most greenhouse kits come with glass pre-cut and ready to install once the frame is assembled. If you have to provide your own, use horticultural glass, which is tougher than standard window glass. Rigid plastic panels, which are sometimes used as an alternative to glass, are light and easy to install but lack the heat-retaining quality of glass and can become cloudy with age.

If possible, locate your greenhouse in a corner of the garden that is exposed to sunlight but sheltered from strong winds. Avoid locating it under trees; they will take away precious sunlight and make the glazing dirty.

Garden centres and greenhouse suppliers sell a wide variety of accessories, such as staging, shelves, heaters, louvred windows and blinds. One of the most useful devices is an automatic ventilator, which opens and shuts the window according to a pre-set temperature.

4

A Roomy All-Purpose Structure

If your car lacks shelter, if your basement is cluttered with tools and garden equipment, or if someone in the family needs a studio or workshop that will not fit in the house, the best solution may be a large outbuilding that can serve almost any purpose except as living quarters. With the help of a few ingenious professional techniques, you can set up a handsome structure that will make life easier for you and increase the value of your property. A raft foundation *(pages 104–109)* eliminates the need for costly forms or masonry skills; pre-cut stud walls *(pages 110–115)* can be built on the ground and erected as a unit, and prefabricated trusses *(left)*, which require no tricky rafter cuts or ridge beam, make the installation of a sloping roof a simple process.

When planning a substantial structure of this type, consider the requirements that its use will create. A garage needs a drive, a path, an area in which to turn the car round and perhaps a side door as well as a main entrance. If you plan to store garden tools in it, you will want a door that provides easy access to the garden. A studio or workshop should have windows, and you may want an attic for storage. Consult your local gas, electricity and water boards about preparing the structure for the installation of their services.

Sketch front and side views of the building on graph paper to determine whether the building will harmonize with the main house and surrounding property. You may wish to plan the roof pitch and overhang of a new structure to match those of the house or of other outbuildings. If you suspect that the building may interfere with a prized view or block sunlight essential to the wellbeing of a garden, you can check by hanging a series of sheets on lines stretched between poles to create the effect the building will have on your property.

You will need a building permit and planning permission. Submit diagrams and sketches describing the type of foundation, wall construction and roof design that you propose. And set up an inspection schedule well in advance so that work will not be delayed. Do not begin work until you have received written permission to go ahead.

Make a list of materials needed for each of the three stages of the job—foundation and slab, stud-wall framing and roof framing—and arrange delivery times that will tie in with your working schedule. If you order all the materials at once for staggered deliveries, you can usually get a contractor's discount—which may sometimes reduce the cost of the building materials by 10 to 20 per cent.

A Special Slab Combining Floor and Foundation

For a sizeable but lightweight building, the simplest type of base is a raft foundation—that is, a concrete slab cast as a unit round a skeleton of reinforcing steel and wire mesh, with its edges turned down into trenches. The turned-down rim supports both the concrete slab and the walls above it, and also protects the slab from any earth movement. The builder need not pour conventional footings, or lay a foundation wall of concrete block, since both footings and foundation are provided by the turned-down rim of the slab.

The slab's most distinctive feature, its turned-down rim, is also its main limitation. The rim requires trenches that are not much wider than the blade of a shovel, but that are still deep enough to meet footing requirements for your area. Digging a trench that meets these specifications may not be possible in some areas because of soil conditions. If your local building department advises against a raft foundation, instead use a deep concrete footing and block wall similar to those described on pages 54–58.

In all likelihood, you will need the advice and consent of your local building department on other aspects of the slab and the building that rises above it. Planning permission is usually required for any structure that is large enough to need a raft foundation, and out-buildings must be located a minimum distance from property lines and also from the main building. As a general rule, before you undertake to pour a large slab, you must submit a rough map of your property to your building inspector, showing the main building and the proposed addition.

A slab as large as the one illustrated on these pages (about 56 square metres and 150 mm thick) requires 10 to 11 cubic metres—or two lorry-loads—of concrete.

Prepare an area for the delivery lorry to off-load the concrete by laying down plastic sheeting as close to the site as possible, and make sure you have at least three helpers on hand—it takes about 25 wheelbarrow-loads to shift a single cubic metre of concrete. Coordinate your helpers so that while some are bringing concrete to the site, others are laying the concrete bay by bay. Some companies will mix concrete on your property as you require it, thereby eliminating the problem of moving and laying large amounts of ready-mixed concrete before it becomes unworkable, after about three hours.

When staking out the site and preparing the profile boards, an automatic level (page 10) will enable you to establish lines and angles both quickly and accurately. You will also need a long tape measure, and a cutter to prepare the reinforcing rods for the trench.

Laying Out the Forms

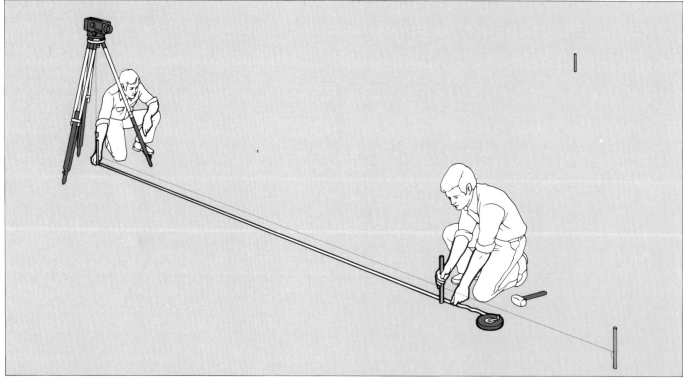

1 Finding the building lines. Drive in stakes to mark the two corners at one side of the slab. Use an automatic level to set a third stake at a right angle (page 12, above); string a line to this stake from the stake beneath the level, and measure along the line with a tape to locate the third corner (above). Drive in a stake there, set the level above it and repeat the operation to find the fourth corner. Check that the diagonals between the corners are equal, then run a boundary of string about 100 mm off the ground round all the corner stakes.

2 **Building profiles.** Drive in three 100 by 50 mm stakes about 500 mm outside the strings at each corner and nail 150 by 25 mm boards, each 1500 mm long, to the stakes to form a right angle; set the tops of the boards about 250 mm above the ground. (A sledge hammer or a large brick makes a solid backing for nailing.) Drive in a 50 by 25 mm sighting stake just outside each set of profiles so that the sighting stakes stand slightly higher than the profiles.

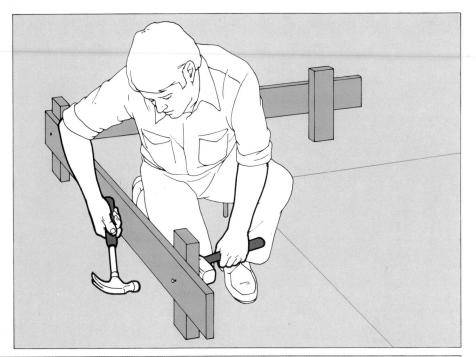

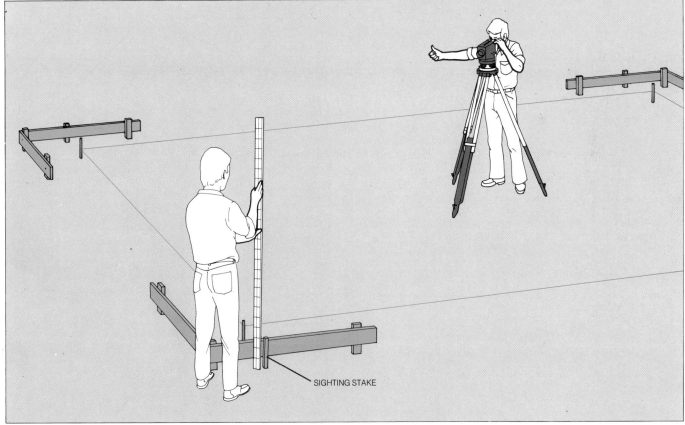

SIGHTING STAKE

3 **Levelling the profiles.** Place the automatic level at the centre of the building site and ask a helper to hold a 2 metre staff next to one of the sighting stakes outside the profiles. Sight through the level at the staff, note the measurement and sub- tract 150 mm from the reading. At each sighting stake, ask your helper to raise the staff until you see this adjusted figure in the level, then mark the sighting stake at the bottom of the staff. Drive the profile stakes down until the profile tops meet the marks on the sighting stakes; lay a level on the profile tops to see that they are even. String lines between the profiles directly above the lines that run between the corner stakes (*Step 1*). Remove the corner stakes and strings.

Building a Raft Foundation

1 **Placing level forms.** For each section of forms, nail three 400 mm-long 50 by 25 mm stakes to a 2400 mm length of 150 by 50 mm timber. Set the inner face of the forms along the string lines and drive the stakes into the ground until the top of each form is level with the string line. Nail the forms together at the corners and nail a 300 by 150 mm plywood backing between stakes at the points where the form boards butt together.

Drive a 100 by 50 mm bracing stake 300 mm behind every form-board stake. Nail two 50 by 25 mm braces between each bracing stake and form-board stake, one on the ground, the other diagonally *(inset)*.

2 **Preparing the ground.** Remove the topsoil from the area enclosed by the form boards. Dig a trench 300 mm wide and 300 mm deep—deeper if required by the district surveyor—along the inside of the forms, then slope the inner side of the trench at a 30 to 45-degree angle.

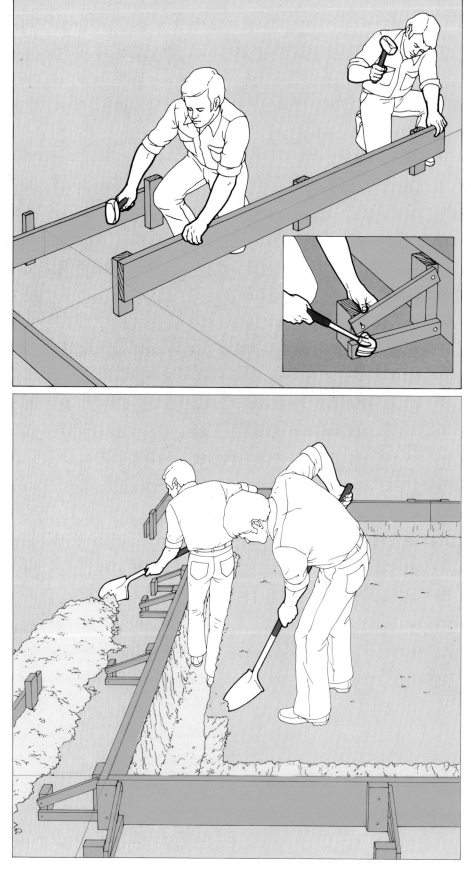

3 **Laying the damp-proof membrane.** Spread broken hardcore over the central slab area to replace the removed topsoil. Cover this with a 25 mm blinding layer of sand, making sure that no sharp fragments of hardcore protrude. Unroll sheets of 1000-gauge polythene over the entire slab area, following the contour of the trenches and lapping the polythene over the form tops by about 150 mm. Overlap adjoining sheets by 150 mm and fold the polythene to fit neatly into the trench corners. Do not secure the polythene sheets to the form boards; they must be left free to move so air pockets cannot be trapped under the foundation when the concrete is poured.

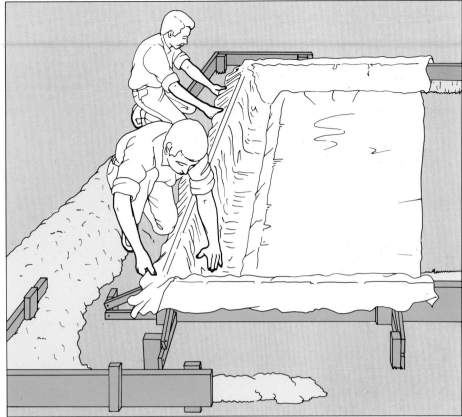

4 **Reinforcing the trenches.** Bend and cut lengths of 10 mm reinforcing rod to form hooked trapezium shapes that will lie 50 mm in from the sides and bottom of the trench. The top side of the hook should extend 500 mm into the central slab area. Set one hook 300 mm from each corner and set others at 1 metre intervals. Thread four lengths of rod horizontally through the hooks and secure them to the corners of each hook with tie wire. If you use rods shorter than the trenches, overlap their ends and tie them together. Wire together the projecting ends of the hooked rods where they meet at corners (*right*).

5 **Reinforcing the slab.** Lay sheets of 6 mm 200 by 200 reinforcing mesh over the slab area, extending the edges of the mesh half way across the trenches and overlapping adjacent sheets by 200 mm. Use tie wire to fasten together overlapping sheets and to attach the mesh to the hooked rods in the trenches.

Prepare sole plates of pressure-treated timber for installation *(Step 7, below)* by drilling 15 mm holes every 1500 mm, and 300 mm from each end, of lengths of 100 by 50 mm timber. Prepare enough sole plates to extend round the rim of the slab, remembering to allow for door openings.

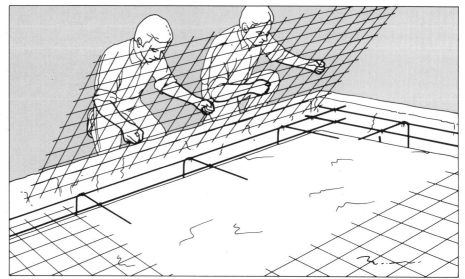

6 **Starting to concrete.** Divide the slab area into three bays with two lengths of 75 by 50 mm timber. Position offcuts of timber under the mesh to bring the tops of the dividing boards level with the top of the form, and drive wedges between the form and the ends of the dividing boards. Pour concrete into one end bay. As you do so, have your helpers lift and shake the mesh and trench reinforcement until there is a 50 mm layer of concrete underneath the mesh and in the trenches. Fill the bay with concrete until it rises about 10 mm above the top of the forms. Then, using a 150 by 50 mm board as a tamping beam, compact and level the first bay *(right)*.

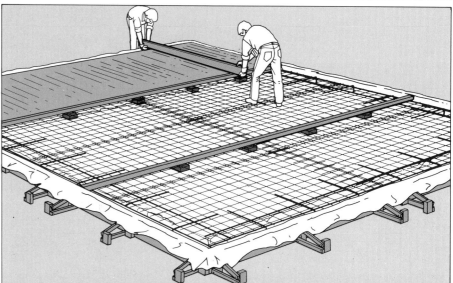

7 **Installing the sole plates.** While your helpers fill and tamp the second outer bay, install a sole plate along the completed side of the slab. Run 10 mm anchor bolts 200 mm long through the holes in the sole plates, fit each threaded bolt end with a washer and a nut and set the plates on the wet concrete, flush with the edge of the slab. Work the bolts down into the concrete, tapping the threaded ends with a wooden mallet if necessary.

As soon as the second bay has been completed, install another end sole plate. Then remove the dividing boards and pour just enough concrete along the outer forms of the middle bay—about 450 mm—to enable you to install the remaining sole plates.

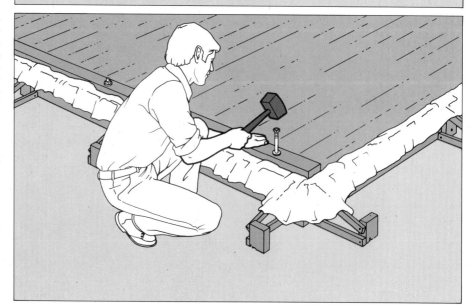

8 Finishing the outer bays. Wait until the surface water has evaporated and the concrete is firm enough to walk on. Working from one end of the bay to the other, smooth the surface of the concrete with a steel float, keeping its leading edge raised about 5 mm. If the bay is too wide for you to reach to the inside edge from outside the form, construct a bridge using a ladder, a scaffold board and bricks and blocks as supports. Take care not to damage the damp-proof membrane.

9 Completing the slab. While a helper finishes the second bay with a float, start to fill the middle bay with concrete, leaving an uncovered area small enough for you to tamp and finish from outside the form. Working from the hardening concrete in the outer bays, compact the middle bay with a tamping beam. When the surface water has evaporated, bridge the covered part of the middle bay with a ladder and board and smooth the concrete with a steel float *(right)*. Remove the bridge, then fill, tamp and finish the remaining area, working from outside the form.

Sprinkle the entire surface of the slab with water, cover with sheets of polythene, and let the concrete cure for three days or more before removing the forms.

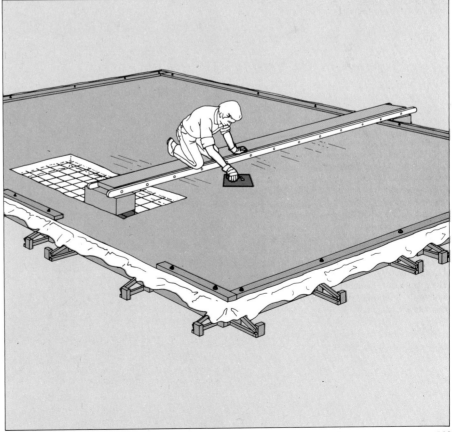

Sturdy Walls Nailed Flat and Tilted Up

Stud walls provide a sturdy framework suitable for any structure from a shed to a house. The principles of stud-wall construction have been standard ever since sawmills began trimming timber to uniform dimensions: vertical studs spaced evenly are nailed to horizontal head plates, each wall is tilted upright section by section and the studs are toenailed to a sole plate. At each opening the roof load is carried by a horizontal header—generally two wide boards nailed together to serve as a beam the same thickness as the studs— that is supported at its ends by posts or studs. The method is the same for any large structure—a garage *(below)*, a workshop with windows and a side door, or a capacious barn with a loft.

To prepare for a job of this magnitude you will need to draw a set of plans—to submit to the building inspector when you have received planning permission and to refer to as you work. Start by drawing a simple floor plan on graph paper; indicate the overall dimensions of the structure, which walls the roof will bear on, the distance between the centre of each opening and the nearest corner of the building, and the size of each rough opening (usually specified by the manufacturer of the finished door or window). Then draw head-on views—what architects call elevations—of the walls with openings; mark the height of the walls, the height and span of each opening and the sizes of the studs, posts and headers that will support the roof.

Use the plan to determine exactly what materials you need when you order timber. Studs—generally 100 by 50 mm, cut to length at the timber yard—are usually spaced 400 mm apart. The 100 by 50 mm head plates should be straight pieces of carcassing timber at least 4200 mm long; shorter pieces or warped timber will make the wall sections difficult to align. The headers in a non-loadbearing wall can be made from timber as small as 150 by 50 mm, but for long spans in load-bearing walls you will need carcassing timber 225 to 275 mm wide by 50 mm. All timber should be pressure-treated, to protect against rot and insects, and provided with a flame-retardant finish. Use galvanized fixings throughout to prevent corrosion.

Precision is important when constructing exterior walls because they support the entire roof. When you mark stud locations for two parallel walls, you should start the layout for each from the same end of the building; this means that the walls will then be mirror images of each other and the roof will bear evenly on them. Make sure that the rough openings and the spacing between studs are correct—even a minor layout mistake can result in huge problems once the walls are up. You should also take pains to plumb the walls accurately and to brace them firmly. The temporary braces must hold the entire structure rigid while the trussed rafters are put in. When the roof has been sheathed, remove the braces one at a time as you apply the wall cladding.

You can build a large structure with ordinary household tools, but a few professional ones will ease the work considerably. The 100 mm round-wire nails that this type of construction requires can be driven in more easily by a 550 to 600 gram hammer than by one with the standard 450 gram head. And you can use a heavy brass or steel plumb bob to check the corners of the walls, rather than try to shield a lightweight bob from the wind.

How the walls fit together. In this typical two-car garage—a rectangle 7.2 metres by 6 metres—the horizontal sole plate is fastened to the foundation with anchor bolts *(page 108, Step 7)*. The studs are nailed to the sole plate and to the lower layer of head plates; the second layer of head plates are nailed to the first to tie the walls together at the corners and at the joints in the first layer. Temporary diagonal bracing holds the corners plumb until the roof and wall sheathing are installed; braces nailed to stakes hold the walls in line with the corners.

The continuous 300 by 100 mm header, spanning the two 2400 mm door openings and the wall between them, is easier to install than independent headers for each opening. The 100 by 100 mm posts that support the header hold it tight against the head plate so that no spacers or short cripple studs are needed. Horizontal 100 by 50 mm noggings nailed between the studs add rigidity to the structure and provide a nailing surface for exterior cladding.

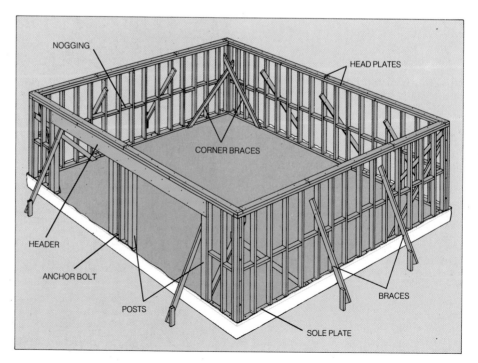

Preparing the Plates

1 Marking the sole plates. Drive a nail part of the way into the sole plate of one of the side walls, 375 mm from the outside edge of the back corner. Hold a combination square against the nail, keeping the nail between the square and the back corner, then square a line across the sole plate. Place a scrap of timber the same thickness as one of your studs along this line and draw a second, parallel line along its opposite edge. Mark an X between the two lines. Hook a long tape measure over the nail and ask a helper to hold the tape taut on the sole plate. Mark the sole plate for studs at 400 mm centres all along the wall.

Lay out studs for the other side wall in the same way, starting from the same end of the building; similarly lay out the back wall and the two front walls outside the door openings.

2 Laying out the head plates. Get a helper to hold one of the head plates against the sole plate so that their ends line up at the corner. With the combination square, transfer the layout marks made in Step 1 to the head plate. Then mark across both plates at the centre of the last stud mark on the head plate *(right)*; cut off the head plate along the mark, so that the joint will fall directly above a stud, and line up the next section of head plate with the mark on the sole plate.

Transfer marks to the remaining sections of head plate in the same way; when you reach the corner of the building, make sure the last section of head plate is at least 2400 mm long and cut it off in line with the end of the sole plate.

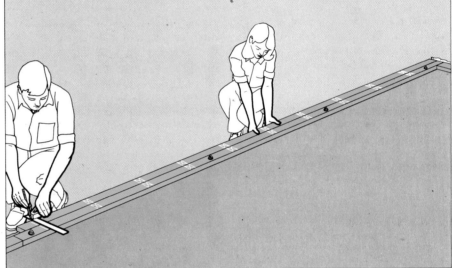

3 Laying out the garage doors. Measure from the outside edge of the sole plates at the front corner to locate the centre of each garage door opening; then measure from the centre line to locate each edge of the opening exactly *(right)*. With a hand-saw, cut off any portion of the sole plate that extends past the edge. To lay out the opening for the garage doors, draw lines across the sole plates at either side, the thickness of the posts from the edges of the opening, and mark Xs on the sole plates for 100 by 100 mm posts. Draw a line across both the head and sole plates an additional 50 mm along and mark an X on each for the full-length studs that will run alongside each post.

At the centre wall between the two openings, mark an X for a 100 by 100 mm post at each end of the sole plate, and then mark for a stud between them *(inset)*.

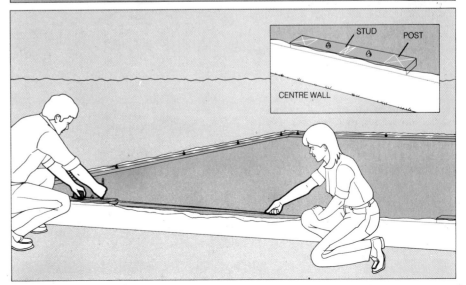

111

Raising the Walls

1 **Nailing the wall together.** Set studs on edge near each layout mark on the sole plate of one wall and set the head plate above them with its layout marks facing the studs. Line up each stud with a layout mark on the head plate, hold it in place by standing on it and drive two 100 mm round-wire nails through the plate into the stud.

If a stud is located at a joint in the head plate, make sure only half of the plate bears on it and angle the nails towards the centre. If a stud is laid out over an anchor bolt, notch the bottom end of the stud to fit over the bolt.

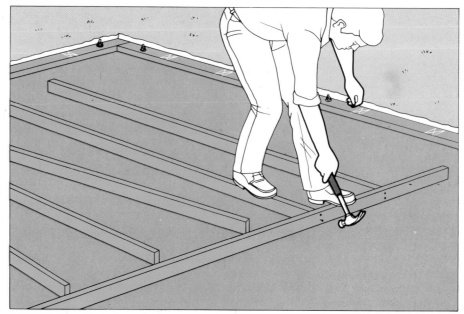

2 **Preparing the corners.** Sandwich three 100 by 50 mm blocks between two of the straightest studs you can find, making sure the blocks line up with the sides of the studs and do not protrude beyond their ends, and fasten the sandwich together from each side with 100 mm round-wire nails. Nail this corner post to the end of whichever head plate runs past the adjacent one at the corner *(inset)*. To complete the corner, nail another straight stud to the end of the adjacent head plate when you assemble the adjacent wall. The stud will be nailed to the post to tie the two walls together.

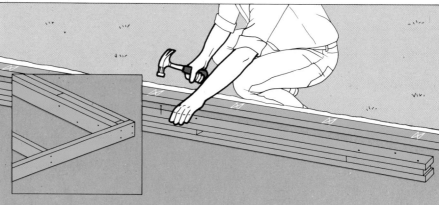

3 **Tilting the wall upright.** With one helper for every 2400 mm of wall, lift the head plate from the slab and tilt the wall upright. Set the studs on the marks on the sole plate, check with a level to make sure the wall is roughly vertical and brace it every 2 metres with 100 by 50 mm pieces of timber *(page 76, Step 3)*. Toenail each stud to the sole plate with 75 mm round-wire nails, two from one side and one from the other.

Lay out and erect the other side wall and the back wall in the same way.

4 **Posts to support the header.** Nail together the two front walls on the slab, using head plates that hang over the door opening by at least 900 mm. Then fasten 100 by 100 mm posts to the studs nearest the door with staggered 100 mm round-wire nails every 250 mm. To determine the length of the posts, subtract the thickness of the sole plate from the height of the rough opening specified by the door manufacturer. Erect and brace the front walls *(Steps 1–3)*.

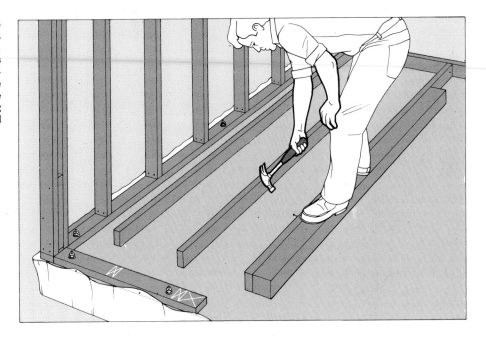

Aligning and Bracing the Framework

1 **Plumbing the corners.** Drive a nail part of the way into the top of the head plate near the corner stud and dangle a plumb bob from the nail, with the tip of the bob level with the top of the sole plate. Make a temporary brace by cutting 45-degree angles on both ends of a long 100 by 50 mm piece of timber. Rest one end of the brace on the slab next to the sole plate of the adjoining wall, and nail the other end to the side of the corner stud near the head plate of the wall you are plumbing; make sure the brace does not protrude beyond the stud. Remove any temporary braces near the corner and ask a helper to move the wall that is to be plumbed gradually towards the vertical. When the tip of the plumb bob lines up with the edge of the sole plate, get a second helper to nail the bottom of the corner brace to the sole plate of the adjoining wall *(right)*.

Move the plumb bob to the other side of the corner and brace the adjoining wall in the same way; then brace the other corners.

2 **Lining up the walls.** Temporarily nail a 100 by 50 mm block to the side of the head plate near each end of a wall. Drive nails part of the way into the head plate behind the blocks and stretch a string tightly between the nails, using the blocks as spacers to hold it out from the top plate. Use a scrap of 100 by 50 mm timber as a gauge to measure the gap between the taut string and the head plate at each brace; get your helpers to unfasten the brace from the stud; move the wall until the string barely touches the block and nail the brace securely to the stud. Line up the other walls in this way.

Cut lengths of 100 by 50 mm timber to serve as noggings between the studs along all the walls of the structure. Secure them half way up the walls in a staggered pattern so that the ends of adjacent noggings are not aligned *(inset)*. Drive two 87 mm round-wire nails through the studs into the end of each nogging; toenail the last nogging of each side to the corner posts. If noggings are to serve as nailing surfaces for cladding, toe-nail them without the stagger to the studs, or use angle brackets.

100 × 50 mm SPACER

3 **Adding the second head plate.** Place a 100 by 50 mm plate on top of the original head plate, starting at a corner where the head plate of the adjoining wall runs through to the outside edge. One end of the new plate should overlap the original head plate of the adjoining wall; cut the other end so that it falls at least 1200 mm away from joints in the lower head plate. Nail the new plate to the lower one with staggered 75 mm round-wire nails, one between every pair of studs. If the new plate is not straight, force it into line by toenailing it through its side into the top of the lower plate.

To tie the corners securely together, get your helpers to push the studs of adjacent walls towards the corner; when the original head plates meet, drive two 100 mm round-wire nails through the end of the new plate into the old head plate of the adjoining wall.

Install the other new head plates in the same way, lapping the joints between the lower plates and tying the corners together *(inset)*. Then nail the temporary corner braces *(page 113, Step 1)* to every stud they cross.

Bridging Large Openings

1 Building the header. Measure between the layout marks for the studs on either side of the garage doors and cut two straight pieces of 275 by 50 mm timber to this length. Apply a thin, zig-zag bead of waterproof adhesive to one of the boards and glue the two together. Secure them from both sides with staggered 75 mm round-wire nails set 250 mm apart.

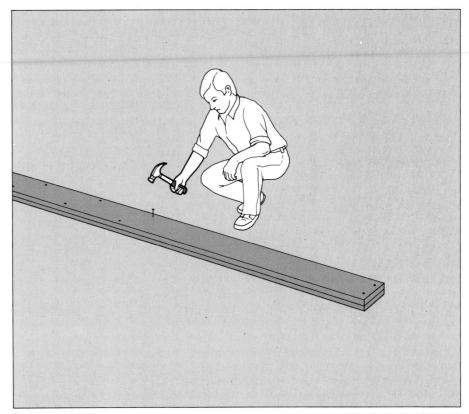

2 Lifting the header into place. With two helpers, lift the header and slide it on to the posts. Get the helpers to hold the ends in place while you nail the stud alongside the post to the header end and nail the head plate to the top of the header, using 100 mm round-wire nails. Fasten the header to the post, stud and head plate with framing anchors. If the header does not fit snugly against the head plate, nail a plywood spacer or short cripple studs on top of it. Finish the head plate with a length of 100 by 50 mm timber and add a second head plate *(opposite page, Step 3)*.

3 Building the centre wall. Cut two 100 by 100 mm posts and one stud to fit tightly between the header and the sole plate of the centre wall. Set the posts and stud in position and toenail them to the sole plate. Check one post with a level, adjust it until it is perfectly vertical and toenail it to the header. Measure between this post and the other at the sole plate, transfer the measurement to the bottom of the header and make a layout mark there; do the same for the stud. Toenail the post and the stud to the header, then fasten both of the posts to the header with framing anchors.

Ready-Made Trusses to Support the Roof

The fastest and cheapest way to frame a roof for a simple rectangular structure is to use pre-manufactured trussed rafters, known simply as "trusses". They eliminate the need for heavy structural joists and rafters, for the tedious cutting of rafters at complex angles, and for the dangerous job of erecting a ridge board.

The modern truss, based on building techniques that go back to 2500 B.C., resembles the ones widely used for the wooden bridges of the 19th century. It is composed of three principal timbers: two top chords that form the slope of the roof, and a tie beam that spans the distance between the exterior load-bearing walls. The three corners of a truss are joined with metal or plywood gussets. Additional members, known as webs, are fitted between the top chords and the tie beam to support the top chord and transfer stress to the tie beam and to the exterior load-bearing walls. This design feature helps prevent the walls from bowing outwards.

Because the average truss for a 6 to 9 metre span is made of 100 by 50 mm timber, it can be lifted into place with little effort, and a whole roof can be completed in hours—a job that might take days with traditional roofing methods. And because these standardized prefabricated trusses can span as much as 10 metres without centre supports, they provide unencumbered interior space by eliminating the need for interior load-bearing walls.

When ordering trusses, you need to specify the span between the exterior walls of the building, the length of the overhang and the type of end cut—either plumb or horizontal—that you desire. You must also specify the pitch of the roof. Regulations regarding the shape of roofs may vary from one region to another. You will need to consult your local planning officer or truss manufacturer for this information. If the pitch of the roof is not regulated by code, trusses that match the pitch and overhang on your house generally give a pleasing appearance to your new structure.

Order the two end trusses with webs spaced 400 mm apart, so that cladding can be nailed to these trusses before they are put up *(page 119, Step 6)*. And have an opening framed in the end trusses so that you can install a window to provide light and ventilation.

Trusses come in a variety of styles. If you plan to build a catwalk above the tie beams for storage, order a truss that has no centre web rather than the type shown on these pages. If you are planning to store heavy objects on such a platform or hang objects from the trusses, order heavy-duty trusses.

To erect trusses, you will need two adjustable scaffolds 2 metres high—these are available at most hire shops. You will also need two framing anchors *(page 78, inset)* for each truss and a large supply of galvanized nails. Trusses rely on sheathing rather than the traditional ridge board for stability. Buy enough 12 mm chipboard to cover the roof—allowing 10 per cent extra for waste. This chipboard must be weatherproofed with roofing felt when the structure is completed *(page 91)*. Buy 100 by 25 mm timber—two 2400 mm-long sections for every three trusses—which you will use to hold the trusses in place until the sheathing is installed on the roof *(pages 120–121, Steps 4–5)* and then will reuse to space the tie beams of the trusses *(page 122, Step 3)*.

You will need at least two helpers to lift and roll the trusses into place. When lifting the trusses, always carry them in a vertical position with one worker at each end and one in the middle to support the tie beam.

Preparing the Walls and the End Trusses

1 **Marking positions for trusses.** Standing on a scaffold, use a tape to measure 625 mm from the side wall and make a mark, square across the front wall's head plate. Put an X and a second line on the side-wall side, to indicate the exact position of the truss.

Lay out the rest of the trusses at 600 mm centres, using the first mark as a starting point. Then lay out the other wall, starting your layout from the same side wall. If the trusses are properly laid out, every second truss should fall directly over a stud in a wall like the one shown here.

2 **Fastening the framing anchors.** Place the framing anchors on the head plate so that their raised edges align with the marks on the head plate. Nail the framing anchors to the head plate with 37 mm galvanized nails.

3 **Laying out the overhang.** Overhang is not essential but improves appearance and weather protection. Nail lengths of 100 by 50 mm timber, long enough to provide the desired overhang, to the outside faces of the head plates of the side walls, and flush with the tops of the head plates. Mark the length of the overhang from the front wall on each 100 by 50 mm length, then tie a string line tautly between the marks *(below)*.

4 **Fastening the nailer.** Nail 2.5 to 3 metre lengths of 100 by 50 mm timber over the head plates of the side walls, flush with the outward edge of the front wall. Space them back the thickness of the truss from the outside edge, using a 100 by 50 mm block on edge to maintain the spacing while nailing *(right)*.

Prepare the temporary braces for the end trusses by cutting 1200 mm strips of sheathing and nailing them to four 2400 mm studs *(inset)*.

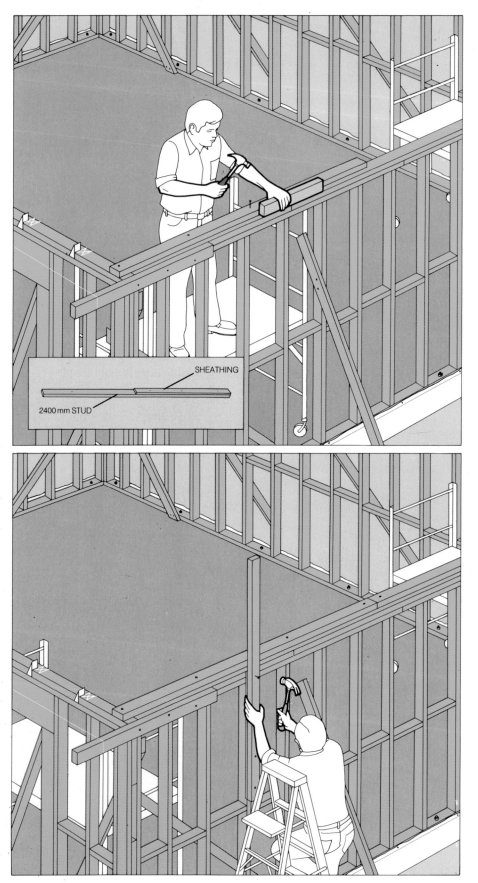

SHEATHING

2400 mm STUD

5 **Erecting the braces.** Nail two braces *(Step 4, inset)* to each side wall about a third of the way in from the front and back walls. Position each brace so that the top edge of the sheathing is flush with the head plate of the wall and the rest of the brace sticks up above the head plate far enough to provide support for the end truss.

6 Cladding the end trusses. Lay the end trusses on the ground and cover them with 2440 by 1220 mm sheets of exterior-grade chipboard, aligning the short edge of the chipboard with the heel and tie beam of the truss. Snap a chalk line along the top chord of the truss and the heel and then cut the chipboard along the chalk line. Nail the cladding to the truss. Finish cladding the truss in the same way. Cut an opening for a window with a jigsaw.

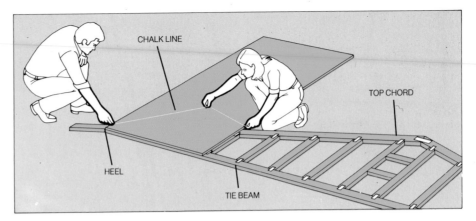

Raising the Roof

1 Hoisting the end truss. With two helpers, carry an end truss upside down into the building and from a scaffold lift one end until the top chord rests on the head plate *(right)*. Then, with a helper standing on another scaffold, set the other end of the truss on top of the opposite head plate.

2 Rolling a truss. With two helpers on scaffolds holding the truss in position, wedge a length of 100 by 50 mm timber into the peak of the truss and rotate the truss into an upright position.

When the peak is upright, walk the truss over to the side wall and set it between the 100 by 50 mm nailer and the braces. Align the overhang with the string line on the front wall and nail the braces to the top chords of the truss.

3 **Securing the end truss.** Standing on a ladder outside the building, drive 100 mm oval lost-head nails through the cladding and into the truss and nailer at 300 mm intervals.

Roll the second truss up, align it with the string line and secure it to the head plates by nailing it to the framing anchors.

4 **Bracing the top chords.** Nail a 100 by 25 mm brace to the end truss, its end flush with the outside of the top chord. Align the second truss at a distance equal to the truss spacing, mark the brace and nail it to the truss. Nail another 100 by 25 mm brace on the other side of the ridge.

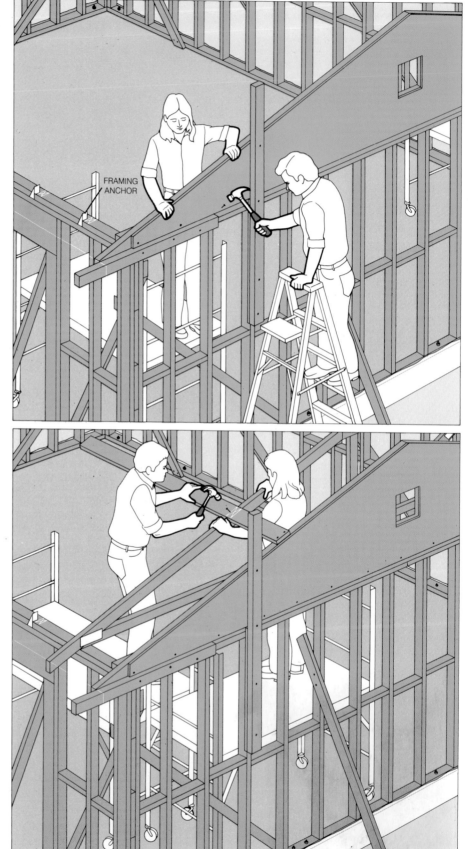

FRAMING
ANCHOR

5 **Bracing the remaining trusses.** Roll up, anchor and brace all the other trusses except the last four, bracing them as you go. Attach the remaining end truss. Roll the last three trusses up, then walk them into place *(below)* and secure them.

Completing the Job on Top

1 **Plumbing the end truss.** Nail a 4800 mm brace made of 100 by 50 mm timber between the window framing of the end truss and a 100 by 50 mm stake firmly anchored outside the building. Loosen the temporary truss braces and adjust the brace while a helper plumbs the end truss with a long level. When the truss is plumb, nail the brace to the stake.

Set up the scaffolds along the side walls and, with a helper, snap chalk lines along the upper chords of the trusses 1200 and 2400 mm from the overhang, to lay out the chipboard sheathing.

2 **Sheathing the trusses.** Tack the corners of a 2440 by 1220 mm piece of chipboard to the end truss, its edge flush with the outside edge. While a helper rechecks the end truss for plumb, tack the corners of the chipboard on the centre line of the fifth truss. Nail the chipboard down with 37 mm clouts spaced every 150 mm.

After sheathing the bottom 1200 mm of the roof, remove the 100 by 25 mm braces and sheathe the next 1200 mm, starting the first sheet of chipboard 1200 mm from the end truss so that joints will be staggered.

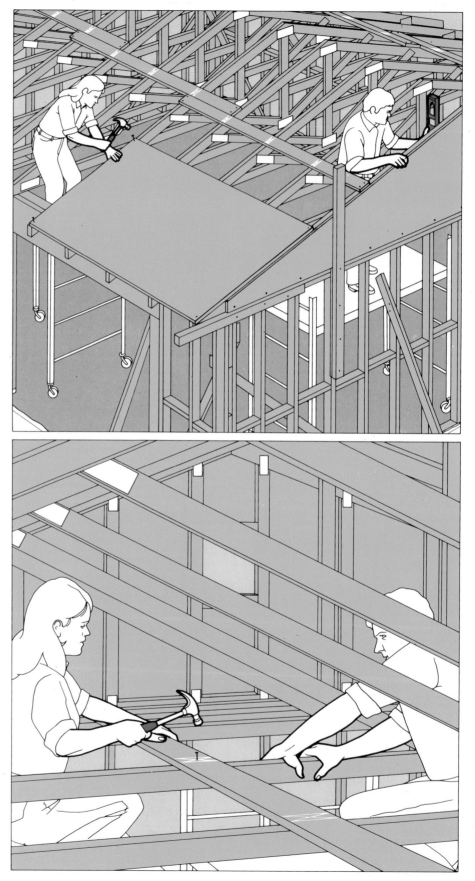

3 **Stabilizing the trusses.** Connect the tie beams of all trusses by nailing to them the 2400 mm lengths of 100 by 25 mm bracing removed from the roof. Align the tie beams with the marks on the bracing *(page 120, Step 4)*, so that the tie beams are spaced exactly as far apart as the top chords. In high-wind areas, nail additional 100 by 25 mm diagonal braces to the webs between the top chord of each end truss and the tie beam of the fifth truss from each side wall.

Cladding with Chipboard Panels

For an outdoor structure like the one shown on the preceding pages, you can clad the walls with shiplap or feather-edged boards, but exterior-grade plywood, or chipboard as here, will save you time. Use panels 18 mm thick; 2440 by 1220 mm is a convenient size. Since building regulations require you to provide at least half an hour of fire resistance, choose fire-retardant chipboard. This contains ground vermiculite crystals, which release a protective layer of steam when exposed to fire.

The illustrations on this page show chipboard panels nailed vertically to the studs. If you plan to set the panels against the studs horizontally, put noggings between the studs wherever adjoining panels butt up against each other, to serve as a nailing surface *(page 114, Step 2)*. Fit the chipboard panels over the turned-up damp-proof membrane along the edge of the slab, extending them about 25 mm below the base of the sole plates.

To make sure that the panels are water-tight, use a Z-cap flashing between the end-truss panels and the side-wall panels. Then use sealant *(Step 2)* to caulk between the panel joints. Protect the corners of the building with corner moulding and use galvanized nails to prevent rust stains. Finally, apply a coat of exterior-grade polyurethane varnish to improve the weather-resistance of your cladding.

1 **Nailing the cladding.** Slip a Z-shaped piece of flashing *(inset)* under the back side of the truss panel and then hold a chipboard panel under it while a helper nails the panel to the studs. Put nails every 150 mm round the edges of the panel and every 300 mm along the intermediate studs. Continue attaching the chipboard panels in this fashion, butting them over the studs but leaving 2 mm vertical gaps between them to allow for expansion.

2 **Weatherproofing the cladding.** Caulk the gaps between the chipboard panels with a polyurethane or silicone sealant. Cover the exposed edges of the chipboard at the corners of the building with strips of right-angled corner moulding *(inset)* or, if you prefer, simply butt lengths of 75 by 25 mm and 100 by 25 mm timber at corners.

Picture Credits

The sources for the illustrations in this book are shown below. Credits for the pictures from left to right are separated by semicolons, from top to bottom by dashes.

Cover: John Elliott. 6: John Elliott. 8, 9: Drawings by Walter Hilmers Jr. 10–13: Drawings by Oxford Illustrators Ltd. 14–17: Drawings by Peter McGinn. 18, 19: Drawings by Oxford Illustrators Ltd. 20–25: Drawings by Fred Bigio from B-C Graphics. 26–31: Drawings by Walter Hilmers Jr. 32: Fil Hunter. 34–39: Drawings by Nick Fasciano. 40–45: Drawings by John Massey. 46: Drawings by Oxford Illustrators Ltd. 47: Drawings by John Massey. 48: Drawing by Oxford Illustrators Ltd.—drawing by John Massey. 49: Drawings by John Massey. 50, 51: Drawings by Oxford Illustrators Ltd. 52: Drawings by Eduino Pereira. 53: Drawing by Oxford Illustrators Ltd.—drawing by Eduino Pereira. 54, 55: Drawings by Walter Hilmers Jr. 56: Drawings by Oxford Illustrators Ltd. 57, 58: Drawings by Walter Hilmers Jr. 59: Drawings by Oxford Illustrators Ltd. 60: Drawings by Walter Hilmers Jr. 61, 62: Drawings by Eduino Pereira. 63: Drawings by Raymond Skibinski. 64: Library of Congress. 65: Drawings by Nick Fasciano. 66: Fil Hunter. 68: Drawing by Peter McGinn. 69: Drawing by Oxford Illustrators Ltd.—drawings by Peter McGinn. 70: Drawings by Oxford Illustrators Ltd. 71–73: Drawings by Peter McGinn. 74: Drawing by Fred Bigio from B-C Graphics. 75: Drawing by Oxford Illustrators Ltd.—drawing by Fred Bigio from B-C Graphics. 76, 77: Drawings by Fred Bigio from B-C Graphics. 78, 79: Drawings by Nick Fasciano. 80–82: Drawings by John Massey. 83–85: Drawings by Raymond Skibinski. 86–89: Drawings by Eduino Pereira. 90, 91: Drawings by Gerry Gallagher. 92: Drawings by Peter McGinn. 93, 94: Drawings by Gerry Gallagher. 95: Drawings by Oxford Illustrators Ltd. 96, 97: Drawings by Peter McGinn. 98, 99: Drawings by Gerry Gallagher. 100, 101: Drawings by Margaret King. 102: Fil Hunter. 104–109: Drawings by Oxford Illustrators Ltd. 110–123: Drawings by Fred Bigio from B-C Graphics.

Acknowledgements

The editors would like to thank the following: Ray Adams, London; John Bungey, Sydney, Australia; Capricorn Spiral Designs Ltd., London; Ralph Clucas, Sydney, Australia; Deans Blinds, London; Véronique Despreaux, London; Fawden and Jenkins, Ewell, Surrey; Fergus Fleming, London; Tim Fraser, Sydney, Australia; Halls Homes and Gardens Ltd., Paddock Wood, Kent; Hamleys, London; Elizabeth Hodgson, London; Vicki Robinson, London; Sally Rowland, Saffron Walden, Essex; Mr. R. Wainwright, TRADA, London; Peter White, London; Wild Heerbrugg, Lordswood, Kent.

Index/Glossary

Metric Conversion Chart

Approximate equivalents—length

Millimetres to inches		Inches to millimetres	
1	1/32	1/32	1
2	1/16	1/16	2
3	1/8	1/8	3
4	5/32	3/16	5
5	3/16	1/4	6
6	1/4	5/16	8
7	9/32	3/8	10
8	5/16	7/16	11
9	11/32	1/2	13
10 (1cm)	3/8	9/16	14
11	7/16	5/8	16
12	15/32	11/16	17
13	1/2	3/4	19
14	9/16	13/16	21
15	19/32	7/8	22
16	5/8	15/16	24
17	11/16	1	25
18	23/32	2	51
19	3/4	3	76
20	25/32	4	102
25	1	5	127
30	1 3/16	6	152
40	1 9/16	7	178
50	1 31/32	8	203
60	2 3/8	9	229
70	2 3/4	10	254
80	3 5/32	11	279
90	3 9/16	12 (1ft)	305
100	3 15/16	13	330
200	7 7/8	14	356
300	11 13/16	15	381
400	15 3/4	16	406
500	19 11/16	17	432
600	23 5/8	18	457
700	27 9/16	19	483
800	31 1/2	20	508
900	35 7/16	24 (2ft)	610
1000 (1m)	39 3/8		

Metres to feet/inches		Yards to metres	
		1	0.914
2	6' 7"	2	1.83
3	9' 10"	3	2.74
4	13' 1"	4	3.66
5	16' 5"	5	4.57
6	19' 8"	6	5.49
7	23' 0"	7	6.40
8	26' 3"	8	7.32
9	29' 6"	9	8.23
10	32' 10"	10	9.14
20	65' 7"	20	18.29
50	164' 0"	50	45.72
100	328' 1"	100	91.44

Conversion factors

Category	Unit	Equivalent
Length	1 millimetre (mm)	= 0.0394 in
	1 centimetre (cm)/10 mm	= 0.3937 in
	1 metre/100 cm	= 39.37 in/3.281 ft/1.094 yd
	1 kilometre (km)/1000 metres	= 1093.6 yd/0.6214 mile
	1 inch (in)	= 25.4 mm/2.54 cm
	1 foot (ft)/12 in	= 304.8 mm/30.48 cm/0.3048 metre
	1 yard (yd)/3 ft	= 914.4 mm/91.44 cm/0.9144 metre
	1 mile/1760 yd	= 1609.344 metres/1.609 km
Area	1 square centimetre (sq cm)/ 100 square millimetres (sq mm)	= 0.155 sq in
	1 square metre (sq metre)/10,000 sq cm	= 10.764 sq ft/1.196 sq yd
	1 are/100 sq metres	= 119.60 sq yd/0.0247 acre
	1 hectare (ha)/100 ares	= 2.471 acres/0.00386 sq mile
	1 square inch (sq in)	= 645.16 sq mm/6.4516 sq cm
	1 square foot (sq ft)/144 sq in	= 929.03 sq cm
	1 square yard (sq yd)/9 sq ft	= 8361.3 sq cm/0.8361 sq metre
	1 acre/4840 sq yd	= 4046.9 sq metres/0.4047 ha
	1 square mile/640 acres	= 259 ha/2.59 sq km
Volume	1 cubic centimetre (cu cm)/ 1000 cubic millimetres (cu mm)	= 0.0610 cu in
	1 cubic decimetre (cu dm)/1000 cu cm	= 61.024 cu in/0.0353 cu ft
	1 cubic metre/1000 cu dm	= 35.3147 cu ft/1.308 cu yd
	1 cu cm	= 1 millilitre (ml)
	1 cu dm	= 1 litre see **Capacity**
	1 cubic inch (cu in)	= 16.3871 cu cm
	1 cubic foot (cu ft)/1728 cu in	= 28,316.8 cu cm/0·0283 cu metre
	1 cubic yard (cu yd)/27 cu ft	= 0.7646 cu metre
Capacity	1 litre	= 1.7598 pt/0.8799 qt/0.22 gal
	1 pint (pt)	= 0.568 litre
	1 quart (qt)	= 1.137 litres
	1 gallon (gal)	= 4.546 litres
Weight	1 gram (g)	= 0.035 oz
	1 kilogram (kg)/1000 g	= 2.20 lb/35.2 oz
	1 tonne/1000 kg	= 2204.6 lb/0.9842 ton
	1 ounce (oz)	= 28.35 g
	1 pound (lb)	= 0.4536 kg
	1 ton	= 1016 kg
Pressure	1 gram per square metre (g/metre^2)	= 0.0295 oz/sq yd
	1 gram per square centimetre (g/cm^2)	= 0.228 oz/sq in
	1 kilogram per square centimetre (kg/cm^2)	= 14.223 lb/sq in
	1 kilogram per square metre (kg/metre^2)	= 0.205 lb/sq ft
	1 pound per square foot (lb/ft^2)	= 4.882 kg/metre^2
	1 pound per square inch (lb/in^2)	= 703.07 kg/metre^2
	1 ounce per square yard (oz/yd^2)	= 33.91 g/metre^2
	1 ounce per square foot (oz/ft^2)	= 305.15 g/metre^2
Temperature	To convert °F to °C, subtract 32, then divide by 9 and multiply by 5	
	To convert °C to °F, divide by 5 and multiply by 9, then add 32	

Phototypeset by Tradespools Limited, Frome, Somerset
Colour reproduction by Grafascan Limited, Dublin, Ireland
Printed and bound by Artes Gráficas Toledo, SA, Spain

D. L. TO:920-1986

tuscany

tuscany

a culinary journey of discovery

PAMELA GWYTHER

Marks and Spencer p.l.c.
PO Box 3339
Chester CH99 9QS

shop online
www.marksandspencer.com

ISBN: 1-84461-663-0

Printed in China

Produced by the Bridgewater Book Company Ltd

Photography: Laurie Evans
Home economist: Carol Tennant

Notes for the Reader
This book uses both metric and imperial measurements. Follow the same units of measurement throughout; do not mix metric and imperial. All spoon measurements are level: teaspoons are assumed to be 5 ml, and tablespoons are assumed to be 15 ml. Unless otherwise stated, milk is assumed to be full fat, eggs and individual vegetables such as potatoes are medium and pepper is freshly ground black pepper. Recipes using raw or very lightly cooked eggs should be avoided by infants, the elderly, pregnant women, convalescents and anyone suffering from an illness. The times given are an approximate guide only.

Picture Acknowledgements
The publisher would like to thank the following for permission to reproduce copyright material: Owaki – Kulla/Corbis (pages 6 to 11, edges), Desgrieux/PhotoCuisine/Corbis (page 30), Envision/Corbis (page 39), Roulier/Turiot/photocuisine/Corbis (page 46), Linda Lewis/PictureArts/Corbis (page 52), Kevin Black/StockFood Creative/Getty (page 53), Marianna Day Massey/ZUMA/Corbis (page 60), J. Riou/photocuisine/Corbis (page 73), Ed Young/Corbis (page 74), Gregor Schuster/zefa/Corbis (page 75), Photonica /Getty (page 76) and Rita Maas/PictureArts/Corbis (page 86).

Contents

Introduction

Italy has several provinces, each one endowed with individual characteristics and culture derived from its own particular climate, geography and history. The provinces range from the hot, dry areas in the south to the cooler foothills of the Alps in the north. None, though, has as rich and diverse a climate, culture and cuisine as Tuscany.

A little history

The region of Tuscany first came to prominence in the eleventh century BC, as the home of the Etruscan civilization. Later, under the influence of the Romans, it became known as Tuscia. This powerful heritage developed Tuscany into the world's most prominent culture in the second millennium. Michelangelo, Dante, Cellini and Brunelleschi, among other renowned figures, led an artistic and literary revolution, supported by the wealth and power of dynasties such as the Medicis. Florence became the symbol of these riches, although other towns such as Siena, Pisa and Lucca all rose to importance.

Tuscany first gained popularity with the British in the nineteenth century, attracting literary giants such as Shelley, Byron, the Brownings and Tennyson. They were followed in the twentieth century by Virginia Woolf and E M Forster, all of whom found the unique culture and climate a welcome alternative to the cold damp of their homeland.

Tuscan cuisine

It is this temperate climate, coupled with a region abundant in the produce of both soil and sea, that has created the characteristic cuisine of Tuscany. From the green hills topped with poplars and cypresses to the flatter Maremma region in the south comes a rich variety of meat and game, including the ever-popular wild boar. The best beef in Italy comes from the Chiano, south of Arezzo, and the Tyrrhenian Sea provides a fine range of fish for Tuscan fish stews or the lightly fried *Fritto Misto di Mare*.

History has left its mark on Tuscan food, too. For example, Siena's famous panforte cake owes its origins to the spices brought in visiting caravans from the Orient in the Middle Ages. Tomatoes originated from Sicily but were brought to Tuscany by Garibaldi's soldiers in the nineteenth century. The same century saw maize being imported for the first time, which is now a staple food, particularly in the form of polenta.

Classic ingredients

Olive oil

Some Tuscan products are, however, timeless. The region still produces some of the best olive oil in Italy – fragrant, rich, slightly peppery, but full of health-promoting properties. It is low in cholesterol compared to other fats, and rich in vitamin E, so therefore beneficial for the skin. The lower the acidity, the better the oil, and the best comes from around Lucca, although each of Tuscany's ten sub-regions has its own speciality. Extra-virgin olive oil must be below 1 per cent in acidity and is ideal for drizzling on salads or onto bruschetta and over grilled meats and fish. Higher levels of acidity make for a cheaper olive oil, which is best used for frying.

The olive harvest takes place from October to December, when the trees in the olive groves have nets spread under them to catch the ripe fruit as the trees are shaken. But the highest quality and most expensive oils are made from hand-picked fruit to avoid damage to the trees, which can sometimes live for over a century. The fruit is pressed twice to extract the oil – a first light and cold pressing followed by a more forceful squeezing under pressure and at a higher temperature. The first extraction is the most highly prized and priced.

Beans

Another timeless and typical Tuscan staple is the bean. There are many varieties, the oldest being black-eyed beans, which were grown in Roman times. In the fifteenth century, as trading links developed with the recently discovered New World, white or cannellini beans were first imported. They proved highly suitable for the rich Tuscan soil and warm temperate climate. Borlotti beans are also popular, available in shades of red, cream and magenta. Beans constitute a low-cost, high-protein, energy-providing staple ingredient. Their mild flavours and textures go well with strongly flavoured yet simple Tuscan dishes.

Pork and ham

Pork and ham are also key ingredients in their many dried, cured forms. There are two main varieties. *Prosciutto* (which means 'dried') is a thinly sliced, tasty ham that has been preserved through air-drying, and is best eaten with vegetables or fresh Tuscan bread and olive oil. *Salami* (which means 'salted') is also dried but is made from finely cut pork combined with spices, herbs and salt. Both prosciutto and salami should be dried for at least six months before eating. *Pancetta* is another variety, made from belly pork. Sausages are also very popular in the region.

The importance of simplicity…

Tuscan culinary skills have been preserved by generations of cooks and in the many small, family-run restaurants. With such a wide range of premium raw materials available to them, a style has evolved that is based on simplicity, using only the freshest ingredients, in season and of magnificent quality, unadorned with anything to mask their basic excellence. Consequently, the bold, natural flavours come through, undisguised by sauces or cream and butter, and accompanied only perhaps by fresh bread. Cooking methods are kept simple, too. Meat and poultry are generally just roasted or grilled, preferably over an open wood fire. Vegetable dishes are served separately and are often a meal in themselves.

Bread, locally baked or home-made to traditional recipes and generally unsalted so that the flavours of the main dishes are not compromised, is the main accompaniment. For those new to it, *pane sciocco* or *toscano* (Tuscan bread) can be something of a challenge. It is truly bland, but the lack of salt has an interesting history. Salt was an essential economic and medicinal commodity in times gone by. Indeed, many English words have their roots in the Latin word for salt, *sal*. 'Salary', for example, derives from the Latin *salarium argentums* or salt money. In the sixteenth century, the Papacy tried to impose a salt tax on the fiercely independent Tuscans, who retaliated by refusing to put salt in their bread. Having done so, they discovered how well it helped maintain the flavours of the wonderful raw materials in the rest of the meal, so have continued the habit to this day. However, the bread is not completely without flavour – the unique taste of the natural yeasts and the artisan flours captured in hand-made breads cooked in wood-fired ovens can be captivating. The main shapes are the round *bozza*, the long *filone* and the more familiar *ciabatta*. Sometimes, flavours are added in the form of nuts, olives, onions or spices.

...and the seasons

A Tuscan cook typically has to provide two full meals a day
for his or her family, which is another major reason why a
simple approach to meal planning has evolved. It is made
easier by the habit of daily shopping in local markets that are
full of the fresh produce of the season. Tuscan cooks would
not dream of buying and eating fruit or vegetables, meat or
fish outside their natural seasons. And why should they, when
each season brings an abundance of gloriously fresh colours,
textures and flavours?

The countryside begins to awaken in the spring, when
markets fill with fresh young vegetables and salads, including
tender broad beans that can be eaten raw. Both wild and
white asparagus varieties appear, along with a whole range of
artichokes – small and large, green and blue. Green or 'wet'
garlic (garlic that is fresh from the ground) and spring onions,
early rosemary and sage all add their particular flavour to
salads and meats.

Summer sees Tuscany's most prolific natural bounty piled high
in the markets. Tomatoes offer different shapes, sizes and
colours for salads or for preserving or making into a sauce or
paste. Courgettes, peppers and aubergines add vibrant colour
to the market as well as variety to the plate. Carrots, onions
and celery cry out to be chopped and simmered in fragrant
olive oil. Fine green beans are followed by fresh cannellini
beans and then by the colourful borlotti beans. Aromatic basil,
parsley, oregano and marjoram are just waiting to enhance all
manner of delicious dishes.

Summer is also the prime time for fruit. Sweet cherries and
strawberries start the season, followed by apricots, peaches
and nectarines as the temperature rises. As the heat increases

further, different varieties of melon come to the fore — fragrant cantaloupe varieties for eating with prosciutto, and bigger and juicier watermelons to quench the thirst. Fresh figs and dessert grapes, along with almonds, are served to end the meal.

The coming of autumn signals another change in eating. Mushrooms in a range of varieties — porcini being the most popular — appear and are used to add additional flavour to stews, to add interest to salads and omelettes or for simply grilling with olive oil. It is also the time for truffles. White or black, they are highly prized and hugely expensive yet wonderfully flavoursome and can turn a simple risotto or pasta dish into an extravagant feast. Pumpkins are roasted, made into soups or used to stuff ravioli. Apples and pears of all shapes and flavours abound and are frequently eaten with pecorino cheese and fresh walnuts.

Autumn, too, is the time of the grape harvest. Tuscan wines are as good as the food they accompany so well. Quaffable whites are made from the trebbiano and vernaccia grapes, and are ideal chilled as an aperitif or served with grilled fish. Delightful reds, using the sangiovese grape, are equally palatable with pasta and meat dishes. Particularly famous is Chianti, with the best *classico* coming from the area between Florence and Siena, although even better quality red wine can be found in Montepulciano and Montalcino. A local speciality wine — Vin Santo — embodies all that is best in Tuscan cuisine. It is a sweet wine made from grapes hung in smoky kitchens to concentrate the flavours, and is generally drunk at the end of a meal to round off a magnificent dining experience.

Now that you have discovered a little more about Tuscan cooking, you can look forward to preparing, cooking and enjoying for yourself the many culinary delights that Tuscany has to offer by sampling the full range of recipes that follows.

Starters
and Soups

Antipasti are appetizers and, as the name suggests, the dishes that come before the pasta course. A typical selection could include cold meats or vegetables simply served with a little extra-virgin olive oil.

Antipasti can be either hot or cold depending on the season. Hot dishes could include a grilled slice of bread with a topping. Cold dishes generally are similar to salads, with a vegetable base enhanced by olive oil.

There are three main types of soup. Plain broths are popular, although thicker soups are favoured in cooler weather. Best of all, though, are the really thick varieties, heavy with beans and other pulses or vegetables.

Wild mushroom bruschetta

Bruschetta di funghi

Serves 4

4 slices sourdough bread, such as Pugliese

3 garlic cloves, 1 halved and 2 crushed

2 tbsp extra-virgin olive oil

225 g/8 oz mixed wild mushrooms, such as porcini, chanterelles and field mushrooms

1 tbsp olive oil

25 g/1 oz butter

1 small onion or 2 shallots, finely chopped

50 ml/2 fl oz dry white wine or Marsala

salt and pepper

2 tbsp roughly chopped fresh flat-leaf parsley, to garnish

Bruschetta, like crostini, are grilled or griddled slices of country bread that are rubbed with garlic and drizzled with the very best extra-virgin olive oil. A variety of toppings can then be added, such as this mushroom one.

Toast the bread slices under a preheated grill or in a preheated ridged griddle pan on both sides, rub with the garlic halves and drizzle with the extra-virgin olive oil. Transfer to a baking sheet and keep warm in a warm oven.

Wipe the mushrooms thoroughly to remove any trace of soil and slice any large ones. Heat the olive oil with half the butter in a frying pan, add the mushrooms and cook over a medium heat, stirring frequently, for 3–4 minutes until soft. Remove with a slotted spoon and keep warm in the oven.

Heat the remaining butter in the frying pan, add the onion and crushed garlic and cook over a medium heat, stirring frequently, for 3–4 minutes until soft. Add the wine, stir well and leave to bubble for 2–3 minutes until reduced and thickened. Return the mushrooms to the frying pan and heat through. The sauce should be thick enough to glaze the mushrooms. Season to taste with salt and pepper.

Pile the mushrooms on top of the warm bruschetta, scatter with the parsley and serve immediately.

Bread and tomato soup

Pappa al pomodoro

Serves 6

450 g/1 lb two-day-old crusty
Italian open-textured bread, such
as Pugliese

1 kg/2 lb 4 oz ripe plum tomatoes

4 tbsp olive oil

4 garlic cloves, crushed

500 ml/18 fl oz boiling water

1 bunch of fresh basil

salt and pepper

6 tbsp extra-virgin olive oil, to serve

The simplest of Tuscan soups that relies on really fresh ingredients, this is best made at the height of the summer when the tomatoes are at their sweetest and the basil is at its most fragrant.

Cut the bread into slices and then cubes (you can remove some of the crusts if you wish) and leave to dry out for 30 minutes. Meanwhile, peel the tomatoes (see Cook's Tip) and cut into chunks.

Heat the olive oil in a large saucepan, add the garlic and cook over a medium heat, stirring, for 1 minute without browning. Add the tomatoes and simmer gently for 20–30 minutes until the mixture has thickened.

Add the bread and stir until it has absorbed the liquid. Stir in the boiling water until you have a thick soupy mixture. Season well with salt and pepper (salt quantities will vary according to the type of bread used).

Remove the basil leaves from their stems and tear any large leaves into pieces. Stir the basil into the soup.

Serve warm with a tablespoonful of extra-virgin olive oil sprinkled over each bowl.

Cook's tip

Peel the tomatoes by plunging them into a heatproof bowl of boiling water for 10–15 seconds, then transfer with a slotted spoon to a bowl of cold water. Pierce the skins with a sharp knife and, when cool enough to handle, peel away the skins.

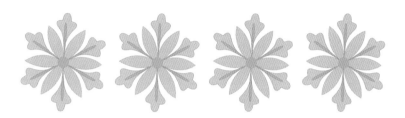

Traditional bean and cabbage soup

Ribollita

Serves 6

200 g/7 oz dried cannellini beans, soaked in cold water overnight

3 tbsp olive oil

2 red onions, roughly chopped

4 carrots, peeled and sliced

4 celery sticks, roughly chopped

4 garlic cloves, roughly chopped

600 ml/1 pint water or vegetable stock

400 g/14 oz canned chopped tomatoes

2 tbsp chopped fresh flat-leaf parsley

500 g/1 lb 2 oz cavolo nero, trimmed and finely sliced

1 small two-day-old ciabatta loaf, torn into small pieces

salt and pepper

extra-virgin olive oil, to serve

This is a traditional peasant Tuscan soup and is very robust. Cavolo nero is now widely available, but if necessary you could use a dark Savoy cabbage.

Drain the beans and put in a large saucepan. Cover with fresh cold water and bring to the boil, skimming off any scum that rises to the surface with a slotted spoon. Reduce the heat and simmer, uncovered, for 1–1 1/2 hours until tender, topping up with water if required.

Meanwhile, heat the olive oil in a large saucepan, add the onions, carrots and celery and cook over a medium heat, stirring frequently, for 10–15 minutes until softened. Add the garlic and cook, stirring, for 1–2 minutes.

Drain the beans, reserving the cooking water, and add half the beans to the vegetable mixture. Pour in the measured water and tomatoes, add the parsley and season well with salt and pepper. Bring to a simmer and cook, uncovered and stirring occasionally, for 30 minutes. Add the cavolo nero and cook, stirring occasionally, for a further 15 minutes.

Put the remaining beans in a food processor or blender with some of the reserved cooking water and process until smooth. Add to the soup. Stir in the bread. The soup should be thick, but add more of the reserved cooking water to thin if necessary. Continue to cook until heated through.

Serve hot with a drizzle of extra-virgin olive oil.

Cook's tip
You can use 400 g/14 oz canned cannellini beans instead of the dried beans to save time. Drain and process in a food processor or blender with a little stock or water until smooth.

Chickpea soup

Zuppa di ceci

Serves 6

400 g/14 oz dried chickpeas, soaked in cold water overnight

2 tbsp olive oil

1 onion, finely chopped

2 garlic cloves, finely chopped

450 g/1 lb Swiss chard, trimmed and finely sliced

2 fresh rosemary sprigs

400 g/14 oz canned chopped tomatoes

salt and pepper

slices of toasted bread, to serve

Chickpeas are another Tuscan staple, used in soups, stews and vegetable dishes. They become stale very quickly, so check the 'use by' date on the packet.

Drain the chickpeas and put in a large saucepan. Cover with fresh cold water and bring to the boil, skimming off any scum that rises to the surface with a slotted spoon. Reduce the heat and simmer, uncovered, for 1–1¼ hours until tender, topping up with water if necessary.

Drain the chickpeas, reserving the cooking water. Season the chickpeas well with salt and pepper. Put two-thirds in a food processor or blender with some of the reserved cooking water and process until smooth, adding more of the cooking water if necessary to give a soup consistency. Return to the saucepan.

Heat the oil in a medium saucepan, add the onion and garlic and cook over a medium heat, stirring frequently, for 3–4 minutes until the onion has softened. Add the Swiss chard and rosemary sprigs and cook, stirring frequently, for 3–4 minutes. Add the tomatoes and cook for a further 5 minutes, or until the tomatoes have broken down to an almost smooth sauce. Remove the rosemary sprigs.

Add the Swiss chard and tomato mixture to the chickpea purée and simmer for 2–3 minutes. Taste and adjust the seasoning if necessary.

Serve in warmed bowls with warm slices of toasted bread on the side.

Chestnut and pancetta soup

Minestra di castagne e pancetta

Serves 4–6

3 tbsp olive oil

175 g/6 oz pancetta, cut into strips

2 onions, finely chopped

2 carrots, peeled and finely chopped

2 celery sticks, finely chopped

350 g/12 oz dried chestnuts, soaked in cold water overnight

2 garlic cloves, finely chopped

1 tbsp finely chopped fresh rosemary

1 litre/1¾ pints good-quality chicken stock

salt and pepper

extra-virgin olive oil, to serve

Sweet chestnuts are gathered in October in the Chianti region of Tuscany. Dried chestnuts or the vacuum-packed variety make this recipe simple to make at home.

Heat the olive oil in a large saucepan, add the pancetta and cook over a medium heat, stirring frequently, for 2–3 minutes until starting to brown.

Add the onions, carrots and celery and cook, stirring frequently, for 10 minutes, or until slightly golden and softened.

Drain the chestnuts, add to the saucepan with the garlic and rosemary and stir well. Pour in the stock, bring to a simmer and cook, uncovered, for 30–35 minutes until the chestnuts are beginning to soften and break down – this thickens the soup.

Season well with salt and pepper and serve immediately in warmed deep dishes with the extra-virgin olive oil drizzled over.

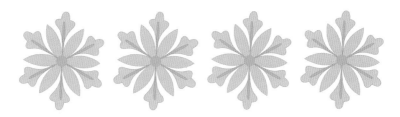

Tuscan summer salad

Panzanella

Serves 4

8 large ripe tomatoes

2 garlic cloves, crushed

6 tbsp extra-virgin olive oil, plus extra to serve

2 tbsp red wine vinegar or balsamic vinegar

225 g/8 oz two-day-old Tuscan saltless bread or other rustic country bread

1 red onion, halved through the root and cut into fine crescent shapes

small handful of fresh basil leaves, coarsely torn into pieces

salt and pepper

This is a traditional simple bread and tomato salad. If you have not made any Tuscan saltless bread, use another rustic country bread such as ciabatta.

Halve the tomatoes and remove and discard the seeds, then cut the flesh into eighths. Put in a sieve over a bowl to collect the juice.

Add the garlic to the tomato juice and season well with salt and pepper. Pour in the oil and vinegar and stir well.

Break the bread up into rough pieces and put in a large bowl. Pour over the tomato juice mixture and gently stir until the bread has absorbed all the juice. Rub the bread between your fingers to break it into smaller pieces, handling it very carefully to avoid breaking it up too much.

Place a layer of the soaked bread in a serving dish and spoon over half the tomatoes and onion. Add another layer of bread and top with the remaining tomatoes, onion and the basil. Cover and leave to stand at room temperature for 1 hour for the flavours to be absorbed by the bread.

Stir well, taste and adjust the seasoning if necessary and drizzle with a little extra oil before serving.

Cook's tip
You can add grilled peppers, capers, anchovies and olives to this salad, but the simple recipe is more traditional.

Ham and salami salad with figs

Insalata di prosciutto, salami e fichi

Serves 6

9–12 ripe figs, depending on size

6 thin slices dry-cured Italian ham

12 thin slices salami

1 small bunch of fresh basil, separated into small sprigs

few fresh mint sprigs

1 small bunch of rocket leaves

2 tbsp freshly squeezed lemon juice

4 tbsp extra-virgin olive oil

salt and pepper

Figs are an integral part of Italian food, not only as a dessert but served, as here, as a starter with cured ham and salami. Make sure that the figs are ripe and soft, as unripe figs are disappointingly lacking in flavour.

Trim the stems of the figs to leave just a short length, then cut the figs into quarters.

Arrange the ham and salami on a large serving platter.

Wash and dry the herbs and rocket and put in a bowl with the prepared figs.

Whisk the lemon juice and oil together with a fork in a small bowl and season well with salt and pepper. Pour over the herbs and salad leaves and carefully turn the figs and leaves in the dressing until they are well coated.

Spoon the figs and salad onto the meat and arrange around the platter.

Artichoke and asparagus salad

Insalata di carciofi e asparagi

Serves 6

6 small globe artichokes

juice of 1 lemon

225 g/8 oz fine asparagus spears

6 tbsp extra-virgin olive oil

70 g/2½ oz pitted black olives

3 anchovy fillets in oil, drained and chopped

2 tbsp chopped fresh flat-leaf parsley

salt and pepper

85 g/3 oz Parmesan cheese, shaved

Artichokes and asparagus are wonderful summer vegetables and are only in season for a short time. Make sure you buy them as fresh as possible to enjoy simply with olive oil or melted butter, or, as here, in a salad.

Trim the stems of the artichokes to 1 cm/ ½ inch in length and cut off the top quarter of the leaves. Bring a large saucepan of water with half the lemon juice added to the boil and add the artichokes. Reduce the heat and simmer for 15–20 minutes until the leaves pull away easily.

Meanwhile, cut off the woody ends of the asparagus and if necessary shave some of the fibrous stalk away. Wipe thoroughly and cook in an asparagus cooker (a tall saucepan that allows the stems to be cooked upright so that the tips are steamed) or simmer in a large frying pan until tender. This should take 5–8 minutes. Drain and leave to cool, then season well with salt and pepper and drizzle with half the oil.

Drain the artichokes, then cool under cold running water and turn upside down to drain. Peel away the tough outside leaves of the artichokes to leave only the tender leaves. Using a sharp knife, cut each artichoke into quarters and remove the hairy choke. Put in a bowl, season well with salt and pepper and add a drizzle of the remaining oil.

Arrange the artichokes and asparagus on individual serving plates and scatter over the olives, anchovies and parsley. Drizzle over the remaining lemon juice and oil and top with the Parmesan cheese shavings before serving.

Cook's tip

If you don't have the time or inclination to prepare fresh artichokes, buy small artichoke hearts in a jar or in cans, drain them and halve – you will need 12.

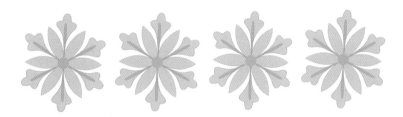

Broad bean and pecorino salad

Insalata di baccelli e pecorino

Serves 6

225 g/8 oz shelled fresh
broad beans

5 tbsp extra-virgin olive oil

2 tbsp freshly squeezed lemon juice

1 tbsp chopped fresh mint

175 g/6 oz young unaged pecorino
cheese, cut into cubes

90 g/3¼ oz rocket leaves

55 g/2 oz aged pecorino or
Parmesan cheese, shaved

salt and pepper

This salad is designed to be enjoyed in May/June when fresh broad beans are at their most tender. If your broad beans are not so young, you will need to remove the outer skins.

If the beans are extremely fresh and tiny, you can serve them raw, but otherwise blanch them for 2–3 minutes in a large saucepan of boiling water. Drain, rinse under cold running water and drain again.

Put the drained beans in a dish, pour over the oil and lemon juice and add the mint. Season well with salt and pepper and mix in the pecorino cheese cubes.

Arrange the rocket leaves on a serving dish and spoon over the bean and cheese mixture. Scatter over the cheese shavings and serve.

Cook's tip
If you use older beans or frozen ones, you will need 50 per cent more beans to allow for the removal of the skins. This gives the salad a really lovely bright green colour.

First Courses

Basic bread in Tuscany is ideally home-baked or produced by a local baker using traditional wood-fired ovens. The loaves are a variety of shapes and types. Tuscan pizzas are thin and the toppings simple.

Pasta is, of course, the staple food of Italy. Two tasty Tuscan examples are included here. Gnocchi is another form of pasta-like food. It can be made from semolina or from potatoes and cooked in the same way. A lighter, vegetable gnocchi is also popular in Tuscany.

Risotto is a rich and delicious dish. It should be made with either arborio or carnaroli rice to produce a creamy texture without losing its bite.

Small Tuscan pizzas

Schiacciate

Makes 4

225 g/8 oz strong white flour, plus extra for dusting

2 tsp easy-blend dried yeast

1/2 tsp salt

1 tbsp olive oil, plus extra for oiling

175 ml/6 fl oz warm water

fresh basil sprigs, to garnish

Topping

140 g/5 oz mozzarella cheese, very thinly sliced

4 slices Italian dry-cured ham, torn into strips

4 ripe plum tomatoes, very finely sliced

salt and pepper

2 tbsp extra-virgin olive oil

These are small, very thin pizzas that can be served as an antipasto or cut into small slices to serve with an aperitif.

Mix the flour, yeast and salt together in a mixing bowl. Make a well in the centre. Mix the olive oil and water together in a jug and pour into the well. Gradually mix the liquid into the flour mixture with a round-bladed knife. Gather the mixture together with your hands to form a soft dough.

Turn the dough out onto a lightly floured work surface and knead for 5–7 minutes until very smooth and elastic. Return the dough to the bowl, cover with a clean tea towel or oiled clingfilm and leave to rise in a warm place for 1 hour, or until doubled in size. Turn out and gently knead again for 1 minute until smooth.

Preheat the oven to 220°C/425°F/Gas Mark 7. Oil 2 baking sheets. Divide the dough into 4 pieces and roll each one into a very thin round. Transfer 2 pizza bases to each prepared baking sheet. Arrange the mozzarella slices on top and then the ham. Top with the tomato slices, season well with salt and pepper and drizzle with the extra-virgin olive oil. Leave to stand in a warm place for 10 minutes, or until slightly risen.

Bake in the preheated oven for 15–20 minutes until golden and crisp. Serve hot, garnished with basil sprigs.

Tuscan saltless bread

Pane toscano

Makes 1 large or 2 smaller loaves

450 g/1 lb strong white flour, plus extra for dusting

1½ tsp easy-blend dried yeast

2 tbsp olive oil, plus extra for oiling

300 ml/10 fl oz warm water

The Tuscans like to eat salty, spicy food such as sausages. This traditional saltless bread is an ideal accompaniment to their highly seasoned food.

Mix the flour and yeast together in a mixing bowl. Make a well in the centre. Mix the olive oil and water together in a jug and pour into the well. Gradually mix the liquid into the flour mixture with a round-bladed knife. Gather the mixture together with your hands to form a soft dough.

Turn the dough out onto a lightly floured work surface and knead for 5–7 minutes until very smooth and elastic. Return the dough to the bowl, cover with a clean tea towel or oiled clingfilm and leave to rise in a warm place for 1 hour, or until doubled in size. Turn out and gently knead again for 1 minute until smooth.

Preheat the oven to 200°C/400°F/Gas Mark 6. Oil 1–2 baking sheets. Shape the dough into 1 large oval or 2 smaller ovals and transfer to the prepared baking sheet or sheets. Cover with a clean tea towel or oiled clingfilm and leave to rise in a warm place for 30 minutes.

Make several slashes in the top of the bread with a sharp knife. Bake in the preheated oven for 30–35 minutes (or 20–25 minutes for 2 loaves). If the bread is getting too brown, reduce the temperature a little. To test that the bread is cooked, turn it over and tap it on the bottom – it should sound hollow. Leave to cool on a cooling rack.

Flatbread with onion and rosemary

Focaccia con cipolle e rosemarino

Makes 1 loaf

450 g/1 lb strong white flour, plus extra for dusting

1½ tsp easy-blend dried yeast

½ tsp salt

2 tbsp chopped fresh rosemary, plus extra small sprigs to garnish

5 tbsp extra-virgin olive oil, plus extra for oiling

300 ml/10 fl oz warm water

1 red onion, finely sliced and separated into rings

1 tbsp coarse sea salt

Focaccia is a very popular flatbread made all over the region. It can be made simply with olive oil or with added flavourings, as here.

Mix the flour, yeast and salt together in a mixing bowl, then stir in the chopped rosemary. Make a well in the centre. Mix 3 tablespoons of the oil and water together in a jug and pour into the well. Gradually mix the liquid into the flour mixture with a round-bladed knife. Gather the mixture together with your hands to form a soft dough.

Turn the dough out onto a lightly floured work surface and knead for 8–10 minutes until very smooth and elastic. Return the dough to the bowl, cover with a clean tea towel or oiled clingfilm and leave to rise in a warm place for ¾–1 hour, or until doubled in size. Turn out and gently knead again for 1 minute until smooth.

Preheat the oven to 200°C/400°F/Gas Mark 6. Oil a baking sheet. Gently roll the dough out to a round about 30 cm/12 inches in diameter – it doesn't have to be a perfect circle; a slightly oval shape is traditional. Transfer to the prepared baking sheet, cover with a clean tea towel or oiled clingfilm and leave to rise in a warm place for 20–30 minutes.

Make holes about 5 cm/2 inches apart all over the surface of the dough with the handle of a wooden spoon. Spread the onion rings over the dough, drizzle with the remaining oil and scatter over the salt. Bake in the preheated oven for 20–25 minutes until well risen and golden brown. Five minutes before the end of the cooking time, garnish with the rosemary sprigs. Transfer to a wire rack to cool for a few minutes, then serve the bread warm.

Cook's tip

Sun-dried tomatoes and chopped olives can be added before the final rising or just scattered on top for extra flavour.

Flat noodles with aubergines and peppers

Pappardelle con melanzane e peperoni

Serves 4–6

2 tbsp olive oil

1 red onion, roughly chopped

2 garlic cloves, roughly chopped

55 g/2 oz pancetta, cut into
1-cm/½-inch pieces

1 large aubergine, cut into
1-cm/½-inch cubes

2 red peppers, deseeded and cut
into strips

125 ml/4 fl oz red wine

400 g/14 oz canned chopped
tomatoes

1 tbsp tomato purée

1 small bunch of fresh basil,
shredded

350 g/12 oz fresh pappardelle

salt and pepper

4 tbsp freshly grated Parmesan
cheese, to serve

Pappardelle with hare (*Pappardelle alla lepre*) is a very traditional Tuscan dish, but given that hare is not easily available, this recipe features the same large ribbon pasta with a rich, thick vegetable sauce.

Heat the oil in a large saucepan, add the onion and garlic and cook over a medium heat, stirring frequently, for 3–4 minutes until starting to soften. Add the pancetta and cook, stirring, for 2–3 minutes until starting to brown. Add the aubergine and red peppers, stir well and cook, stirring occasionally, for 8–10 minutes until softened.

Add the wine, tomatoes and tomato purée and bring to the boil, then reduce the heat and simmer, uncovered, for 4–5 minutes, or until the sauce has thickened and reduced. Season well with salt and pepper and add the basil.

Meanwhile, bring a large saucepan of water to the boil. Add the pappardelle and stir well, return to the boil and cook for 2–3 minutes until al dente or just tender but still firm to the bite. Drain and return to the saucepan, reserving a little of the cooking water.

Pour the sauce into the pasta and stir well, adding the reserved cooking water if necessary – the sauce should be thick but moist.

Serve in warmed dishes with Parmesan cheese to taste.

Penne with sausage sauce

Penne con sugo di salsiccie

Italian sausages are now widely available, as their spicy flavour is well liked. However, if you can't find them, use good-quality pork sausages instead.

Serves 4–6

2 tbsp olive oil

1 red onion, roughly chopped

2 garlic cloves, roughly chopped

6 Italian sausages, skinned and the meat crumbled

½ tsp dried chilli flakes

2 tbsp chopped fresh oregano

400 g/14 oz canned chopped tomatoes

350 g/12 oz dried penne

salt and pepper

2 tbsp chopped fresh flat-leaf parsley, to garnish

3 tbsp freshly grated Parmesan cheese, to serve

Heat the oil in a large saucepan, add the onion and cook over a medium heat, stirring frequently, for 6–8 minutes until starting to brown. Add the garlic and the crumbled sausages and cook for 8–10 minutes, breaking up the sausages with a wooden spoon.

Add the chilli flakes and oregano and stir well. Pour in the tomatoes and bring to the boil, then reduce the heat and simmer, uncovered, for 4–5 minutes until reduced and thickened. Season to taste with salt and pepper.

Meanwhile, bring a large saucepan of salted water to the boil. Add the penne and stir well, return to the boil and cook for 10–12 minutes, or according to the packet instructions, until al dente or just tender but still firm to the bite. Drain well and return to the saucepan.

Pour the sauce into the pasta and stir well.

Serve in warmed dishes, scattered with the parsley and Parmesan cheese to taste.

Potato gnocchi with walnut pesto

Topini con pesto alla noce

Serves 4

450 g/1 lb floury potatoes

55 g/2 oz Parmesan cheese, freshly grated

1 egg, beaten

200 g/7 oz plain flour, plus extra for dusting

salt and pepper

Pesto

40 g/1½ oz fresh flat-leaf parsley

2 tbsp capers, rinsed

2 garlic cloves

175 ml/6 fl oz extra-virgin olive oil

70 g/2½ oz walnut halves

40 g/1½ oz pecorino or Parmesan cheese, freshly grated

Potato gnocchi must be made with floury potatoes or the gnocchi will be sticky and chewy. In order to have very dry potatoes, it is important to cook the potatoes in their skins.

Boil the potatoes in their skins in a large saucepan of water for 30–35 minutes until tender. Drain well and leave to cool slightly.

Meanwhile, to make the pesto, chop the parsley, capers and garlic, then put in a mortar with the oil, walnuts and salt and pepper to taste. Pound with a pestle to a coarse paste. Add the pecorino cheese and stir well.

When the potatoes are cool enough to handle, peel the skins from the potatoes and pass the flesh through a sieve into a large bowl or press through a potato ricer. While still hot, season well with salt and pepper and add the Parmesan cheese. Beat in the egg and sift in the flour. Lightly mix together, then turn out onto a lightly floured work surface. Knead lightly until the mixture becomes a smooth dough. If it is too sticky, add a little more flour.

Roll the dough out on a lightly floured work surface with your hands into a long log. Cut into 2.5-cm/1-inch pieces and gently press with a fork to give the traditional ridged effect. Transfer to a floured baking sheet and cover with a clean tea towel while you make the remaining gnocchi.

Bring a large saucepan of water to the boil, add the gnocchi, in small batches, and cook for 1–2 minutes. Remove with a slotted spoon and transfer to a warmed serving dish to keep warm while you cook the remaining gnocchi.

Serve the gnocchi in warmed serving bowls with a good spoonful of the pesto on top.

Spinach and ricotta gnocchi

Gnocchi di spinaci e ricotta

Serves 4–6

1 tbsp olive oil

500 g/1 lb 2 oz spinach leaves

225 g/8 oz ricotta cheese

115 g/4 oz Parmesan or pecorino cheese, freshly grated

2 eggs, lightly beaten

55 g/2 oz plain flour, plus extra for dusting

freshly grated nutmeg

salt and pepper

Sauce

2 tbsp olive oil

2 shallots, finely chopped

1 carrot, peeled and finely diced

2 garlic cloves, crushed

800 g/1 lb 12 oz canned chopped tomatoes

1 tbsp tomato purée

6 fresh basil leaves, roughly torn into pieces, plus extra whole fresh basil leaves to garnish

This gnocchi is very different to the previous potato recipe. It is very much lighter and healthier because it is made with eggs, cheese and spinach.

Heat the oil in a large saucepan. Add the spinach and cook, covered, for 1–2 minutes until just wilted. Drain through a sieve and leave to cool, then squeeze out as much water as possible with your hands (you can squeeze it in a clean tea towel to ensure that it is very dry).

Finely chop the spinach and put in a bowl. Add the ricotta cheese, half the Parmesan cheese, the eggs and flour and mix well. Season to taste with salt and pepper and add a good grating of nutmeg. Cover and chill in the refrigerator for at least 1 hour.

Meanwhile, make the sauce. Heat the oil in a saucepan, add the shallots, carrot and garlic and cook over a medium heat, stirring frequently, for 3–4 minutes until softened. Add the tomatoes and tomato purée and bring to the boil, then reduce the heat and simmer, uncovered, for 10–15 minutes until the sauce is reduced and thickened. Season to taste with salt and pepper and add the basil leaves. If you like a smooth sauce, pass it through a sieve or process in a food processor or blender.

To shape the gnocchi, flour a plate and your hands thoroughly. Put a dessertspoonful of the spinach mixture into the palm of one hand, roll gently into an egg shape and transfer to a floured baking sheet. Repeat with the remaining spinach mixture.

Bring a large saucepan of water to a simmer, carefully add the gnocchi, in small batches, and cook gently for 2–3 minutes until they rise to the surface. Remove with a slotted spoon and transfer to a warmed serving dish to keep warm while you cook the remaining gnocchi.

Serve the gnocchi in warmed dishes with the sauce poured over the top, garnished with basil leaves and with Parmesan cheese to taste.

Mushroom risotto

Risotto con funghi

Serves 4

55 g/2 oz dried wild mushrooms

250 ml/9 fl oz warm water

6 tbsp olive oil

280 g/10 oz mixed fresh wild or
field mushrooms, thickly sliced

2 garlic cloves, finely chopped

1 tbsp finely chopped fresh thyme

1 onion, finely chopped

350 g/12 oz risotto rice (arborio
or carnaroli)

150 ml/5 fl oz dry white wine

700 ml/1¼ pints hot chicken stock

55 g/2 oz butter

115 g/4 oz Parmesan cheese,
freshly grated

salt and pepper

2 tbsp finely chopped fresh flat-leaf
parsley, to garnish

Mushroom risotto is best made with fresh wild mushrooms when they are in
season, but the addition of dried mushrooms to fresh cultivated mushrooms can
add a wonderful flavour.

Soak the dried mushrooms in the warm water in a small bowl for 10–15 minutes. Drain, reserving the soaking liquid (sieve it thoroughly to remove any grit). Finely slice the drained mushrooms.

Heat half the oil in a large frying pan, add the fresh mushrooms and cook over a low heat, stirring occasionally, for 10–15 minutes until soft. Add the dried mushrooms and garlic and cook, stirring frequently, for a further 2–3 minutes. Add the thyme and salt and pepper to taste, then remove the mushroom mixture from the frying pan and keep warm.

Heat the remaining oil in the frying pan, add the onion and cook over a low heat, stirring occasionally, for 10–12 minutes until soft. Gently stir in the rice and cook, stirring, for 1 minute. Pour in the wine and cook, stirring, until it has all been absorbed. Add the reserved soaking liquid and cook, stirring, until it has all been absorbed.

Keeping the stock at simmering point in a saucepan, add one ladleful to the rice and cook, stirring constantly, until it has all been absorbed before adding the next ladleful. Continue adding the stock in the same way, stirring well to ensure that the rice does not stick to the frying pan, until it has all been absorbed – this should take 15–20 minutes. The rice should be very creamy in texture, though it should also be al dente or tender but still firm to the bite. Season to taste with salt and pepper.

Remove from the heat and gently stir in the mushroom mixture, butter and half the Parmesan cheese.

Serve immediately on warmed plates, scattered with the parsley and with Parmesan cheese to taste.

Polenta with chargrilled vegetables

Polenta con verdura mista griglia

Polenta can be served soft, like mashed potato, to accompany meat and fish. It can also be prepared in a thicker form, as here, which is then grilled and served with a variety of toppings.

Serves 4

Polenta

1 litre/1³/4 pints water

1 tsp salt

250 g/9 oz quick-cook polenta

2 garlic cloves, crushed

¹/2 tsp dried oregano

2 tbsp freshly grated Parmesan cheese

3 tbsp olive oil

salt and pepper

Chargrilled vegetables

1 red pepper, deseeded and quartered

1 yellow pepper, deseeded and quartered

2 red onions, sliced into thick rings

2 courgettes, sliced lengthways into 3–4 pieces

1 small aubergine, sliced across into 8 pieces

3 tbsp olive oil

1 lemon, halved

2 tbsp chopped fresh mixed herbs, such as flat-leaf parsley, rosemary and thyme, to garnish

Bring the water to the boil in a saucepan and add the salt. Pour in the polenta, in a steady stream, stirring constantly. Reduce the heat to low and cook, stirring, for 1 minute, or according to the packet instructions. Beat in the garlic, oregano and Parmesan cheese and season well with salt and pepper.

Use 2 teaspoons of the oil to grease a baking sheet and spoon on the polenta mixture. Spread evenly into a 25-cm/10-inch round, smooth the surface and leave to cool for about 1 hour.

Cut the polenta into 8 wedges and brush with the remaining oil. Cook under a preheated medium–high grill or in a preheated ridged griddle pan over a medium–high heat for 1–2 minutes on each side until golden. Remove and keep warm.

Heat a ridged griddle pan until hot. Brush all the vegetables thoroughly with the oil, add to the griddle pan, in batches, and cook over a medium–high heat for 4–6 minutes, turning occasionally, until marked with golden brown stripes and tender. Remove with a slotted spoon, transfer to a warmed serving dish and keep warm while you cook the remaining vegetables. Squeeze the lemon halves over the vegetables and season well with salt and pepper.

Serve 2 slices of the polenta per person with the chargrilled vegetables on top, scattered with the herbs to garnish.

Cook's tip
A little extra-virgin olive oil can be drizzled over the dish before serving.

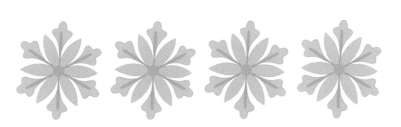

Second Courses

Tuscany is rich in a wide selection of meats, including wild boar, game birds and hare and rabbit. Lamb is also popular, and pigs provide pork, sausages and dried meats. The coastal regions are rich in varieties of fish and shellfish, and inland there are also good freshwater fish.

Chickens are kept both for their eggs and for their flesh. Portions of chicken are often wrapped in pancetta or ham to protect the fragile meat.

Vegetables are an important part of the diet and a huge variety is available all year round. Side dishes of vegetables can be a meal in themselves, particularly with the addition of cheese or dried meats.

Livorno seafood stew

Il cacciucco alla Livornese

Serves 6

4 red mullet fillets

450 g/1 lb monkfish tail

400 g/14 oz cleaned baby squid

3 tbsp olive oil

1 onion, finely chopped

2 garlic cloves, finely chopped

2 fennel bulbs, finely sliced

150 ml/5 fl oz dry white wine

600 g/1 lb 5 oz canned chopped tomatoes

500 g/1 lb 2 oz live mussels, scrubbed and debearded

700 ml/1¼ pints fish stock

18 large raw prawns, peeled and deveined

salt and pepper

To serve

6 slices ciabatta bread, toasted, rubbed with garlic and drizzled with olive oil

2 tbsp finely chopped fresh flat-leaf parsley

This fish stew usually contains at least five varieties of fish, including squid and shellfish. Use whatever is available to give a good mix.

Cut the red mullet fillets into thirds. Cut the monkfish into similar-sized pieces, cutting the flesh away from the tailbone (this can be used to make stock). Cut the squid into thick rings and retain the tentacles.

Heat the oil in a large saucepan, add the onion, garlic and fennel and cook over a medium heat, stirring frequently, for 4–5 minutes until starting to soften. Pour in the wine, stir well and leave to bubble until almost evaporated. Add the tomatoes and bring to the boil, then reduce the heat and simmer, uncovered, for a further 10–15 minutes until the fennel is tender and the sauce is reduced and thickened.

Meanwhile, bring the stock to the boil in a separate large saucepan, add the mussels and cook, covered, over a high heat for 3–4 minutes, shaking the saucepan occasionally, until the mussels have opened. Discard any mussels that remain closed. Sieve the mussels, reserving the stock. Remove half the mussels from their shells, discarding the shells. Keep all the mussels warm.

Add the reserved stock to the tomato mixture and bring to the boil. Add the mullet, monkfish, squid and prawns to the saucepan and cook for 2–3 minutes until tender and the prawns have turned pink. Add the shelled and unshelled mussels and heat through. Season to taste with salt and pepper.

Transfer the stew to individual warmed soup dishes, making sure that the seafood is evenly divided. Serve each dish with the toasted bread slices and sprinkle with the parsley.

Lightly battered and fried fish

Fritto misto di mare

Serves 4–6

18 large raw prawns

225 g/8 oz cleaned baby squid

6 red mullet fillets

light olive oil, for deep-frying

lemon wedges, to serve

Batter

175 g/6 oz plain flour

2 eggs

225 g/8 fl oz cold water

salt and pepper

Mixed fried fish in batter is often served as a starter or a light lunch. The batter should be very light and crisp.

To make the batter, sift the flour into a mixing bowl. Season the flour to taste with salt and pepper and make a well in the centre. Break the eggs into the well and add the water. Gradually beat the eggs and water into the flour to form a smooth batter.

Peel and devein the prawns. Cut the squid into tentacles and rings and the red mullet into small squares.

Heat the oil for deep-frying in a deep-fat fryer, or deep, heavy-based saucepan using a thermometer, to 180–190°C/350–375°F, or until a cube of bread browns in 30 seconds. Dip the seafood in the batter and wipe off any excess. Add to the hot oil, in small batches, and cook for 2–3 minutes until crisp and golden. Remove with a slotted spoon, drain on kitchen paper and keep warm while you cook the remaining seafood.

Pile onto hot plates, season to taste with salt and serve with lemon wedges.

Grilled T-bone steak

Bistecca alla fiorentina

Serves 2

1 large T-bone steak, about
750–800 g/1 lb 10 oz–1 lb 12 oz

extra-virgin olive oil

salt and pepper

mixed salad leaves, to serve

Tuscan beef is famous, particularly the *Chianina* from the Val de Chiani. To ensure a well-flavoured steak, buy meat from a good butcher. Such a delicious treat is often eaten alone, but a simple salad of mixed leaves makes an ideal accompaniment.

Remove the steak from the refrigerator 30 minutes before cooking to return to room temperature.

Light a charcoal barbecue well in advance and add some oak chips to the coals to add flavour. When the coals are grey and very hot, put the steak on the grill rack 10 cm/4 inches above the coals. Cook for 3–4 minutes until well charred. Turn and cook for a further 3–4 minutes until rare but not bloody. Check that it is cooked to your liking. Traditionally, this type of steak is only turned once, but you can cook a little longer on both sides if you like.

Transfer the cooked steak to a chopping board and season well with salt and pepper. Cut the fillet from the bone and the sirloin separately. Thickly slice and serve immediately on warmed plates with a good drizzle of the oil, accompanied by mixed salad leaves.

Cook's tip

If you have a gas barbecue, light and preheat it to high before starting to cook. Alternatively, the steak can be cooked under a preheated hot grill or in a preheated ridged griddle pan over a high heat on the hob.

Roast pork loin

Lonzo di maiale

Serves 6

1.8 kg/4 lb flat piece pork loin, chined (backbone removed) and rind scored

3 garlic cloves, crushed

2 tbsp chopped fresh rosemary

4 sprigs fresh rosemary, plus extra to garnish

225 ml/8 fl oz dry white wine

salt and pepper

cooked seasonal vegetables, to serve (optional)

In Tuscany, whole suckling pigs are roasted in wood-fired ovens. This is a simpler recipe to enable you to cook delicious roast pork at home. Ask your butcher to keep the pork loin in one flat piece and to chine the meat and score the rind for you.

Preheat the oven to 230°C/450°F/Gas Mark 8. Put the pork loin on a work surface, skin-side down. Make small slits in the meat all over the surface. Season very well with salt and pepper (Tuscans like meat highly seasoned). Rub the garlic all over the meat surface and sprinkle with the chopped rosemary.

Roll up the loin and secure 4 rosemary sprigs on the outside with fine string. Make sure that the joint is securely tied. Season the rind with plenty of salt to give a good crackling.

Transfer the meat to a roasting tin and roast in the preheated oven for 20 minutes, or until the fat has started to run. Reduce the oven temperature to 190°C/375°F/Gas Mark 5 and pour half the wine over the meat. Roast for a further 1 hour 40 minutes, basting occasionally with the pan juices.

Remove the meat from the oven and leave to rest in a warm place for 15 minutes before carving. Remove the string and rosemary before cutting into thick slices.

Pour off all but 1 tablespoon of the fat from the roasting tin. Add the remaining wine to the juices in the tin and bring to the boil, scraping up and stirring in any residue from the base of the tin. Spoon over the meat and serve immediately with fresh vegetables, if using, and garnished with extra sprigs of rosemary.

Beef braised in red wine

Stracotto di manzo

Serves 6

3 tbsp olive oil

2 onions, finely sliced

2 garlic cloves, chopped

1 kg/2 lb 4 oz stewing steak, cut into thick strips

2 tbsp plain flour

300 ml/10 fl oz good-quality red wine, such as Chianti

2 fresh sage sprigs

200 ml/7 fl oz beef or vegetable stock

1 tbsp tomato purée

salt and pepper

1 tbsp finely chopped fresh flat-leaf parsley, to garnish

cooked seasonal green vegetables, to serve

Sometimes less-tender cuts of meat are braised in Tuscan cooking, quite often on the hob. But here the beef is cooked in the oven so that it needs little attention.

Preheat the oven to 150°C/300°F/Gas Mark 2. Heat 1 tablespoon of the oil in a large frying pan, add the onions and garlic and cook over a medium heat, stirring frequently, for 6–8 minutes until softened and browned. Remove with a slotted spoon and transfer to a casserole.

Heat the remaining oil in the frying pan, add the steak strips and cook over a high heat, stirring, for 3–4 minutes until browned all over. Sprinkle in the flour and stir well to prevent lumps. Season well with salt and pepper. Reduce the heat to medium, pour in the wine, stirring constantly, and bring to the boil, continuing to stir constantly.

Carefully turn the contents of the frying pan into the casserole. Add the sage, stock and tomato purée, cover and cook in the centre of the preheated oven for 2¹⁄₂–3 hours.

Remove from the oven, discard the sage and taste and adjust the seasoning if necessary. Serve immediately, scattered with the parsley, with some seasonal green vegetables.

Cook's tip
A lamb casserole can be made in the same way. Use lean leg of lamb or shoulder.

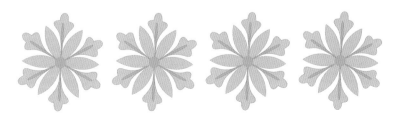

Marinated and grilled leg of lamb

Agnello al rosmarino

Serves 6–8

1 leg of lamb, about 2.25 kg/5 lb

4 garlic cloves, crushed

2 tbsp finely chopped fresh rosemary

finely grated rind and juice of 2 lemons

3 tbsp olive oil

salt and pepper

To serve

green salad

boiled new potatoes (optional)

Tuscan spring lamb is cooked very simply, as it has such a good flavour and texture. Ask the butcher to 'butterfly' it (remove the bone) for you.

Trim any excess fat from the lamb and make small, deep slits in the meat all over the surface. Transfer to a shallow dish and rub all over with the garlic, rosemary and lemon rind. Pour over the oil and lemon juice and season well with salt and pepper. Cover and leave to marinate in the refrigerator, or preferably in a larder or other cool place, for at least 4 hours, or overnight if possible, turning the meat occasionally.

Preheat the grill, or light a gas barbecue and preheat to high or light a charcoal barbecue and leave to burn until the coals are grey and very hot. Remove the meat from the marinade and pat dry with kitchen paper. Season again with salt and pepper and put on the grill rack. Cook for 2 minutes on both sides until sealed, then reduce the heat to medium–high or lift away from the coals and cook for a further 8 minutes on both sides. Test to see if it is cooked to your taste – it should be charred on the outside but still rare in the centre.

Remove from the heat, cover with foil and leave to rest for 15 minutes before carving into long strips.

Serve with a green salad and some new potatoes, if you like.

Stuffed chicken breasts

Involtini di petti di pollo

Serves 4

4 skinless, boneless chicken breasts, about 150 g/5½ oz each

4 thin slices Italian dry-cured ham

4 slices pecorino cheese

4 cooked asparagus spears, plus extra to serve

1 tbsp plain flour

40 g/1½ oz butter

2 tbsp olive oil

150 ml/5 fl oz dry white wine

50 ml/2 fl oz chicken stock

salt and pepper

Chickens are very popular in Tuscany and many families keep their own. Breasts are quickly cooked and here they are stuffed and served with a simple wine sauce.

Put each chicken breast between 2 pieces of clingfilm or inside a polythene food bag and, using a rolling pin, gently beat out until 8 mm/³/8 inch thick.

Season well with salt and pepper and put a slice of ham on top of each chicken breast. Top each with a slice of cheese and an asparagus spear. Roll the breasts up carefully and secure with fine string. Dust with flour and season well with salt and pepper.

Heat 30 g/1 oz of the butter with the oil in a large frying pan. Add the chicken rolls and cook over a moderate heat, turning frequently, for 15 minutes, or until cooked through, tender and golden brown. Remove the string, transfer the chicken rolls to a warmed serving dish and keep warm.

Add the wine and stock to the frying pan and bring to the boil, scraping up and stirring in any residue from the base of the frying pan. Bring to the boil and add the remaining butter. Stir well and leave to bubble until thick.

Spoon the sauce over the chicken and serve immediately, with extra warm asparagus spears.

Cook's tip
You could use Marsala instead of white wine to give a different flavour.

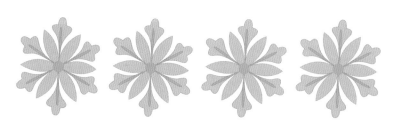

Veal escalopes with Marsala

Scaloppine al Marsala

Serves 2

4 veal escalopes, about 70 g/
2½ oz each

1 tbsp plain flour

3 tbsp olive oil

150 ml/5 fl oz Marsala

salt and pepper

simple risotto or green salad, to
serve

Veal escalopes can be bought ready prepared from the butcher. They are sliced from the tenderloin and then gently beaten to flatten them.

Put each veal escalope between 2 pieces of clingfilm or inside a polythene food bag and, using a rolling pin, gently beat out until 3 mm/ ⅛ inch thick.

Season the escalopes well with salt and pepper and dust with the flour.

Heat the oil in a large frying pan, add the escalopes and cook over a high heat for 1 minute on each side until lightly browned. Add the Marsala and leave the liquid to bubble around the escalopes for 1 minute.

Serve immediately with the pan juices poured over the meat, accompanied by a simple risotto or a green salad.

Stuffed courgettes

Zucchini ripeni

Serves 4

4 round or long courgettes, about 115 g/4 oz each

2 tbsp olive oil

1 onion, finely chopped

2 garlic cloves, finely chopped

4 slices pancetta, diced

55 g/2 oz cherry tomatoes, chopped

2 tbsp pine kernels

4 tbsp fresh white breadcrumbs

2 tbsp shredded fresh basil leaves

55 g/2 oz pecorino cheese, freshly grated

2 tbsp olive oil

2 tbsp freshly grated Parmesan cheese

salt and pepper

Stuffed vegetables can be served as a side dish to meat or fish or as part of an antipasto. The fillings can simply be breadcrumbs and herbs or a meat filling for a more substantial meal.

Preheat the oven to 200°C/400°F/Gas Mark 6. Cut off the top of the round courgettes or cut a slice lengthways from the long courgettes. Scoop out the flesh, making sure that you don't cut through the skin, leaving a shell 5 mm/¼ inch thick. Chop the vegetable flesh and put in a bowl.

Heat the oil in a large frying pan, add the onion and garlic and cook over a medium heat, stirring frequently, for 3–4 minutes until softened. Add the pancetta and cook, stirring, for 2–3 minutes until golden. Add the chopped vegetable flesh and cook, stirring frequently, for 3–4 minutes until the flesh is cooked and the liquid has evaporated.

Add the tomatoes, pine kernels, breadcrumbs, basil and pecorino cheese to the vegetable mixture, mix well and season to taste with salt and pepper. Spoon the mixture into the prepared vegetables and drizzle with the oil.

Arrange the vegetables in an ovenproof dish, cover with foil and bake in the preheated oven for 30–35 minutes until the vegetables are tender. Remove the foil, sprinkle over the Parmesan cheese and bake for a further 10–15 minutes until the cheese is lightly browned. Serve warm.

Variation

Instead of the courgettes, use 2 aubergines, about 250 g/8 oz each. Prepare and cook them in the same way as the courgettes.

Potato and fennel bake

Patate e finocchio al forno

Serves 6

1 kg/2 lb 4 oz potatoes

2–3 fennel bulbs

4 tbsp olive oil

1 onion, finely chopped

2 garlic cloves, crushed

4 fresh sage leaves

150 ml/5 fl oz dry white wine

salt and pepper

Potatoes and fennel are both popular vegetables in Tuscany, and this dish combines them well. Use to accompany grilled meat or fish, or serve on its own as a light lunch.

Preheat the oven to 200°C/400°F/Gas Mark 6. Peel, then finely slice the potatoes. Trim, then finely slice the fennel.

Oil a large gratin dish with half the oil. Layer half the potato slices in the base of the prepared dish and season well with salt and pepper. Scatter over half the onion and garlic and cover with the fennel. Scatter the remaining onion and garlic over and season to taste again with salt and pepper. Tuck the sage leaves into the vegetables. Finish with a neat layer of the potato slices and season to taste again with salt and pepper.

Pour over the wine and drizzle over the remaining oil. Cover the dish with foil and bake in the preheated oven for 30 minutes.

Remove the foil and bake for a further 20–30 minutes until the potatoes are brown and crisp.

Cook's tip
You can use a food processor fitted with a slicer attachment for slicing the potatoes, but a mandolin is the ideal tool to use.

Desserts

Sugar was first imported into Europe from the East through the port of Venice in the Middle Ages, so it is not surprising that northern Italians have a sweet tooth. The tradition of fine pastry cooks started in those times, as feasts were prepared for the rich families of Tuscany.

As in other aspects of Tuscan cooking, local produce is important in desserts. Almonds made into biscotti are traditionally served with the local sweet wine, Vin Santo, into which they are dipped. But for a really indulgent treat, nothing can beat the rich and creamy panna cotta or tiramisù — except, possibly, the recipe here for a truly sinful soft chocolate fondant cake.

Stuffed peaches with amaretto

Peche ripiene

Serves 4

55 g/2 oz butter

4 peaches

2 tbsp soft light brown sugar

55 g/2 oz amaretti biscuits or
macaroons, crushed

2 tbsp amaretto

125 ml/4 fl oz single cream, to serve

Peaches are delicious when fully ripe, simply sliced and served in some sweet white wine. But when they are not quite so ripe, this is a good alternative.

Preheat the oven to 180°C/350°F/Gas Mark 4. Grease a 20-cm/8-inch gratin dish, or a baking dish large enough to hold 8 peach halves in a single layer, with 15 g/¹/2 oz of the butter. Halve the peaches and remove and discard the stones. If you like, you can skin the peaches by adding to a heatproof bowl of boiling water for 10–15 seconds, then transfer with a slotted spoon to a bowl of cold water. When cool enough to handle, peel away the skins.

Beat the remaining butter and sugar together in a bowl until creamy, add the biscuit crumbs and mix well.

Arrange the peach halves, cut-side up, in the prepared baking dish, and fill the stone cavities with the biscuit mixture. Bake in the centre of the preheated oven for 20–25 minutes, or until the peaches are tender.

Pour over the amaretto and serve hot with the cream.

Cook's tip
Apricots can be cooked in the same way when in season – bake in the oven for 10–15 minutes.

Poached pears in Marsala

Pere con Marsala

Serves 4

4 firm dessert pears,
such as Comice

55 g/2 oz caster sugar

2 cinnamon sticks

125 ml/4 fl oz Marsala

125 ml/4 fl oz crème fraîche,
to serve

Pears are a popular fruit in Tuscan cooking and are frequently served as part of a salad, often with walnuts and cheese. Here they are poached until tender in Marsala.

Carefully peel the pears. Cut a slice from the base of each pear and discard, then remove and discard the core from each base with a pointed knife.

Put the prepared pears in a saucepan and add enough water to just cover and the sugar and cinnamon sticks. Slowly bring to the boil over a low heat, stirring until the sugar has dissolved.

Cover and simmer gently until the pears are tender. This will take from 20–40 minutes, depending on their firmness.

Remove from the heat. Remove the pears with a slotted spoon and transfer to a serving dish. Remove the cinnamon sticks.

Return the saucepan to the heat and leave the liquid to bubble for 2–3 minutes until thickened. Stir in the Marsala and pour over the pears.

Serve warm or cover and chill in the refrigerator before serving with crème fraîche.

Soft chocolate cake

Torta al cioccolato

Serves 6–8

280 g/10 oz plain chocolate with at least 72% cocoa solids, broken into pieces

140 g/5 oz unsalted butter, plus extra for greasing

4 eggs, separated

55 g/2 oz caster sugar

25 g/1 oz plain flour

1 tsp vanilla extract

cocoa powder, for dusting

This is a deliciously soft, dark chocolate cake for serving as a dessert. It is like a chocolate fondant, with a velvety smooth centre.

Preheat the oven to 180°C/350°F/Gas Mark 4. Grease and base-line a 20-cm/8-inch springform cake tin with a removable base.

Put the chocolate and butter in a heatproof bowl, set the bowl over a saucepan of barely simmering water and heat until melted. Remove the bowl from the heat and leave to cool for 5 minutes.

Whisk the eggs yolks and sugar together in a mixing bowl with a hand-held electric whisk or hand whisk until thick and creamy. In a separate mixing bowl, whisk the egg whites until thick and glossy.

Fold the egg yolk mixture into the melted chocolate. Sift in the flour and fold in together with the vanilla extract. Gently fold in the beaten egg whites.

Turn the mixture into the prepared tin and bake in the preheated oven for 15–20 minutes. Do not overcook. The top should be firm but the centre still slightly gooey. Remove from the oven and leave to cool, covered, overnight.

Remove the cake tin and peel away the lining paper from the base. Dust the surface of the cake with cocoa powder and serve in slices.

Almond biscuits

Biscotti/Contucci

Makes 20–30

250 g/9 oz whole blanched almonds

200 g/7 oz plain flour, plus 1 tbsp for dusting

175 g/6 oz caster sugar, plus 1 tbsp for sprinkling

1 tsp baking powder

1/2 tsp ground cinnamon

2 eggs

2 tsp vanilla extract

Biscotti get their name from the Italian for 'twice cooked'. The dough is first baked in a log, then cut into slices and baked again.

Preheat the oven to 180°C/350°F/Gas Mark 4. Line 2 baking sheets with baking paper.

Very roughly chop the almonds, leaving some whole. Mix the flour, sugar, baking powder and cinnamon together in a mixing bowl. Stir in all the almonds.

Beat the eggs with the vanilla extract in a small bowl, then add to the flour mixture and mix together to form a firm dough.

Turn the dough out onto a lightly floured work surface and knead lightly. Divide the dough in half and shape each piece into a long, thick log, roughly 5 cm/2 inches wide. Transfer to the prepared baking sheets, sprinkle with sugar and bake in the preheated oven for 20–25 minutes until brown and firm.

Remove from the oven and leave to cool for a few minutes, then transfer the logs to a chopping board and cut into 1-cm/ 1/2-inch slices. Meanwhile, reduce the oven temperature to 160°C/325°F/Gas Mark 3.

Arrange the biscotti slices, cut-sides down, on the baking sheets. Bake in the oven for 15–20 minutes until dry and crisp. Remove from the oven and leave to cool on a wire rack. Store in an airtight container to keep crisp.

Cream dessert with pistachio nuts

Pistachio panna cotta

Serves 6

vegetable oil, for oiling

600 ml/1 pint double cream

1 tsp vanilla extract

4 tbsp caster sugar

2 gelatine leaves

50 g/1¾ oz shelled pistachio nuts

fresh whole raspberries or sliced strawberries, to serve

The cooked cream in this recipe makes it a rich dessert. Here, the addition of chopped pistachio nuts gives a delicious flavour and delicate colour to the dessert.

Oil 6 x 125 ml/4 fl oz dariole moulds or ramekins.

Pour the cream into a saucepan, add the vanilla extract and sugar and stir well. Bring slowly to simmering point over a low heat and simmer gently for 2–3 minutes. Remove from the heat and set aside.

Soak the gelatine leaves in a bowl of cold water for 5 minutes, or until softened. Remove from the water and stir into the hot cream mixture until dissolved.

Process the pistachio nuts in a food processor or grinder until finely ground, or finely chop with a knife. Reserve some of the ground or chopped nuts for the decoration and add the remainder to the cream mixture. Leave to infuse for 15 minutes, then sieve the mixture into a jug. Pour the mixture into the prepared moulds, cover and chill for 3 hours, or overnight until set.

To serve, dip the moulds in hot water for 2 seconds and turn out onto serving plates. Serve with a small portion of raspberries or sliced strawberries and decorated with the reserved ground pistachio nuts.

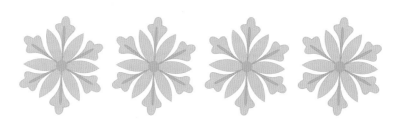

White tiramisù with strawberries

Tiramisù bianco con fragoli

Serves 6

2 eggs, separated

85 g/3 oz icing sugar, sifted

350 g/12 oz mascarpone cheese

6 tbsp full-fat milk

125 ml/4 fl oz Marsala

20 Savoiardi finger sponge biscuits

55 g/2 oz almonds, chopped

55 g/2 oz white chocolate, coarsely grated

fresh strawberries, halved, to serve

Tiramisù translates into English as 'pick-me-up'. It is a rich dessert made using mascarpone cheese mixed with eggs and usually flavoured with coffee. This is a delectable alternative.

Whisk the egg yolks with the sugar in a mixing bowl with a hand-held electric whisk or hand whisk until thick and creamy. Add the mascarpone cheese and whisk into the egg yolk mixture.

Whisk the egg whites in a separate mixing bowl and then fold into the mascarpone mixture.

Pour the milk into a shallow dish and add the Marsala. Dip the biscuits into the milk mixture just long enough to soften, then arrange half the dipped biscuits in the base of a glass or china dish about 23–25 cm/9–10 inches in diameter. Sprinkle over half the almonds. Spread over a third of the mascarpone mixture and top with a layer of the remaining dipped biscuits and the remaining nuts. Spoon the remaining mascarpone mixture over the top and swirl to give an attractive appearance.

Cover with clingfilm and chill in the refrigerator for 2–3 hours.

To serve, remove from the refrigerator and decorate with the white chocolate and halved strawberries.

Cook's tip
For a decorative effect, shave the chocolate from the block with a vegetable peeler to create chocolate curls.

Chocolate and nut cake from Siena

Panforte di Siena

Panforte is famous all over Italy, but originates from Siena. Although the recipe varies, it always contains nuts and candied peel. The addition of chocolate is often made when the cake is served at Christmas time.

Makes 1 cake

175 g/6 fl oz runny honey

140 g/5 oz caster sugar

115 g/4 oz candied lemon peel, finely chopped

115 g/4 oz candied orange peel, finely chopped

100 g/3¹/2 oz ground almonds

100 g/3¹/2 oz whole blanched almonds, roughly chopped

100 g/3¹/2 oz whole blanched hazelnuts, roughly chopped

55 g/2 oz plain flour

2 tbsp cocoa powder

1 tsp ground cinnamon

1/2 tsp ground cloves

a good grating of nutmeg

icing sugar, for dusting

Preheat the oven to 160°C/325°F/Gas Mark 3. Oil and base-line a 20-cm/8-inch round shallow cake tin with a removable base.

Put the honey and sugar in a small saucepan and heat over a low heat, stirring, until the sugar has dissolved.

Put the candied peel in a large mixing bowl and add the nuts. Sift in the flour and cocoa powder and add all the spices. Mix well together. Pour the honey and sugar mixture over the dry ingredients and mix thoroughly together.

Turn the mixture into the prepared tin and press down well so that the surface is smooth. Bake in the preheated oven for 30–40 minutes until firm.

Remove from the oven and leave to cool completely in the tin before removing. Dust heavily with icing sugar before serving in slices. The cake will keep in an airtight container or wrapped in clingfilm and foil for up to 2–3 months.

Apricot ice cream

Gelato di albicocche

Serves 6

500 g/1 lb 2 oz ripe apricots
300 ml/10 fl oz single cream
175 g/6 oz caster sugar
200 ml/7 fl oz full-fat milk
1/2 tsp vanilla extract

A delicious ice cream that is very simple to make. Make sure that you use the ripest apricots when they are in season and at their best.

Halve the apricots and remove and discard the stones. Put the apricots in a food processor or blender and process until smooth.

Whip the cream and sugar together in a mixing bowl using a hand-held electric whisk or a hand whisk until the sugar has dissolved. Whisk in the apricot purée, milk and vanilla extract. Pour into a lidded freezerproof container, cover and freeze for 1 hour.

Remove from the freezer and whisk thoroughly using a hand-held electric whisk or a hand whisk. Re-cover and freeze for a further hour. Repeat the whisking and freezing process until the mixture is almost frozen solid. Whisk a final time, re-cover and return to the freezer until required.

Transfer the ice cream to the refrigerator 15 minutes before serving to soften slightly.

Raspberry water ice

Granita al lamponi

Serves 6

1 lemon
900 g/2 lb raspberries
225 g/8 oz caster sugar
150 ml/5 fl oz Vin Santo

Granita is a frozen water ice that has large ice crystals, giving it a crunchy texture. It is easier to make at home than sorbet.

Finely grate the rind from the lemon into a large jug. Halve the lemon and squeeze out the juice into the jug.

Put half the raspberries with half the sugar in a food processor and pulse until puréed. Pour the purée into a bowl. Repeat with the remaining raspberries and sugar. Add the Vin Santo and stir well.

Pour the mixture into a metal ice tray if available, as the metal will help to freeze the purée more quickly. Otherwise, use a lidded freezerproof container, cover and freeze for 30 minutes.

Remove from the freezer, scrape the set mixture from around the edges using a fork and fork over the mixture. Re-cover and freeze for a further 30 minutes. Repeat the mashing and freezing process every 30 minutes until the mixture is very firm.

Serve immediately straight from the freezer, spooned into chilled bowls. Granita will dissolve quickly once it starts to thaw. It is best served on the day of making, but it will keep, covered, in the freezer for 2–3 days.

Deep-fried pastry ribbons

Cenci

Serves 8

280 g/10 oz plain flour, plus extra for dusting

2 eggs, beaten

2 tbsp light olive oil

2 tbsp caster sugar

2 tbsp Vin Santo

finely grated rind of 1 lemon

4 oranges

light olive oil or sunflower oil, for deep-frying

icing sugar, for dusting

These are crisp little biscuits made by deep-frying strips of pastry that have been cut and tied into ribbons. They are best served hot and are delicious with cold orange segments.

Sift the flour into a large mixing bowl and make a well in the centre. Add the eggs, the 2 tablespoons of oil, sugar, Vin Santo and lemon rind. Mix together with a round-bladed knife to form a dough. Use your hands to knead until smooth. Form into a ball, wrap in clingfilm and chill in the refrigerator for 1 hour.

Meanwhile, working over a bowl to catch the juice, peel and segment the oranges with a sharp knife. Add the segments to the juice, cover and chill in the refrigerator until required.

Divide the pastry in half and roll out one half on a lightly floured work surface to a rectangle about 3 mm/1/8 inch thick. Cover and repeat with the remaining pastry. Using a fluted pastry cutting wheel, cut the pastry into 10-cm x 2.5-cm/4-inch x 1-inch ribbons. Tie a single knot in each pastry strip. Alternatively, for an easier method, cut the pastry into diamond shapes and leave flat.

Heat the oil for deep-frying in a deep-fat fryer, or deep, heavy-based saucepan and using a thermometer, to 180–190°C/350–375°F, or until a cube of bread browns in 30 seconds. Add the pastry ribbons, in small batches, and cook until golden brown. Remove with a slotted spoon, drain on kitchen paper and keep warm while you cook the remaining pastry ribbons.

Dust with icing sugar before serving warm with the orange segments.